To the Union West Library Reference
Department in hopes that caterers and
chefs in the area will be inspired!

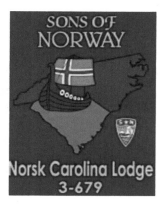

www.norskcarolina.org

https://www.facebook.com/norsk.carolina

FROM CHILDHOOD TO ᵀᴴᴱ BOCUSE D'OR

Geir Skeie Norwegian World Champion From Childhood to the Bocuse d'Or
Copyright © 2010 Skeie Metro Forlag

Production: Metro Branding AS – www.metro.as
Text: Trude Nergaard
Photos: Paal-André Schwital
Graphic design: Runa Fridén

First published 2009 by Skeie Metro Forlag
N-3205 Sandefjord, Norway - www.metro.as

Translated by Rae Walter in association with First Edition Translations Ltd, Cambridge, UK

Printing: Livonia Print SIA, 2010
Paper: Arctic The Matt 150 grams
The book is typeset in: Fedra Sans Display, Fedra Sans Std and Fedra Serif

Printed in Latvia

ISBN 978-82-998105-4-8

I would be pleased to receive comments, suggestions and ideas.
Contact: geir@geirskeie.no
www.geirskeie.no

Wine recommendations:
Lars Martin Moland
Geir Skeie

Other photographs:
Trygve Indrelid: p. 7
Scanpix: p. 35
Rolf Øhman, Aftenposten: p. 76
Veer: p. 14
Norwegian Seafood Export Council/Paal-André Schwital: p. 112, 113
Peter Naghy, Vi Menn: p. 77, 130, 131
Etienne Heimermann: p. 172, 173
Tom Haga: p. 154, 155
Morten Holt, Horeca: p. 152
Shutterstock: p. 34

GEIR SKEIE

NORWEGIAN WORLD CHAMPION

FROM CHILDHOOD TO THE BOCUSE D'OR

SKEIE METRO FORLAG

CONTENTS

6–10 YEARS

MAYBE JESUS LIKED CINNAMON BUNS?

10–16 YEARS

COULD HE BECOME THE WORLD'S BEST CHEF?

16–18 YEARS

THE ART OF MAKING KOMLER IN A HOWLING GALE

- All recipes except cakes and pastries are for 4 persons unless stated otherwise.

- All herbs mentioned are fresh herbs.

- All black pepper used has been toasted. Toast whole peppercorns in a dry pan until they can be crushed with the fingers. This gives a more aromatic pepper, which can be ground later.

- Butter means butter, not margarine.

- Neutral oil is sunflower oil, corn oil, soya oil, rapeseed oil (not cold-pressed) or grape-seed oil, i.e. oil that doesn't have an individual flavour.

- All temperatures are for ordinary domestic fan ovens.

18—22 YEARS

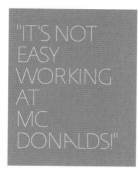

"IT'S NOT EASY WORKING AT MC DONALDS!"

22—28 YEARS

THE MAN WHO CONJURES WITH FLAVOURS

COMPETITIONS

EATING COMPETITIONS AND OTHER CONTESTS

THE MOMENT OF TRUTH

Geir getting close to his "raw ingredients" on the family farm on Fitjar.

THE LAD WITH THE IRON WILL

The grand master of French cuisine is Paul Bocuse in Lyon. In 1987, he created what was to become the world's most important cooking competition, the Bocuse d'Or – a gold cup for the art of fine cooking. The aim was to bring together young, talented chefs from all over the world for a contest in Lyon that would help to launch them on the path to international fame.

Since then, Norwegian chefs have been pre-eminent and won a succession of gold, silver and bronze medals. Only France has a better roll of honour. When Geir became Norway's competitor, half the country expected him to win. He had previously made his mark as the potential favourite by winning top competitions in Norway and not least through his resounding victory in the first Bocuse d'Or Europe in Stavanger in 2008. This victory made him a clear favourite to win gold in Lyon as well.

Norwegian lamb and Norwegian salmon were on the menu in Stavanger. Geir was the first to cook, which is an unenviable position. The judges need reference points and rarely award top marks early on in the competition. Bocuse was officiating as an honorary judge and did not intend to influence the points or judgements. Nevertheless, as soon as he had tasted Geir's dishes, he said to me:
"It will be hard to do better than this!"

And that's how it turned out. None of the 20 nations did better than Geir Skeie from Norway. He exhibited striking precision.

Geir arrived in Lyon on an icy January day after driving across Europe with his practice kitchen in a semi-trailer. 24 nations were preparing for the great world contest. On the stage in the competition hall a storm was brewing. The stands were filled to bursting point. The French wanted a victory. So did the Danes. Everyone wanted victory. The atmosphere in the great hall was electric. A gladiatorial battle was being waged.

Afterwards, when the medals were being distributed and Geir was spraying champagne over the contestants and singing "Ja vi elsker", it was as if an incredible dream was being acted out. Little Norway top in the world's most prestigious cooking contest! A paradox as hard to get over as Norway's highest mountain range. How could it have happened?

In preparation for Lyon, the expression "garage cook" took on a whole new meaning. For six months, Geir had stood in Anders Jahre's old garage at Midtåsen in Sandefjord perfecting his dishes. During this time, he showed his true strength. Some people can invent dishes and be successful with impressive presentations. Some can aim for the roll of honour and work in prestigious places. Some can create a lot of self-publicity and appear all over the media.

But not many people can manage to fulfil expectations and come up with a victory as solid as a triumphal arch. Geir had been preparing for fifteen years. He was determined to win. He was mentally prepared, he knew what he was in for and had set out his every move so he could do everything blindfold.

"It is typical of Norwegians to be good," said Prime Minister Gro Harlem Brundtland during the Winter Olympics in Lillehammer in 1994. She was mainly thinking of skiers and skaters. A Norwegian world champion chef was a sensation. Geir Skeie left the stage with a gold medal round his neck. Amid all the cheering, I didn't manage to tell him that it would be difficult to do better than that!

In this book, Geir shows what he is really in touch with. His recipes are modern and classic at the same time, showing his closeness to nature and to his raw ingredients, and not least his respect for work well done. The most important thing for a chef is to know when to take action in order to get the optimum result. Not too much and not too little. Like all good chefs, Geir has learned how to control the heat.

Maybe it is the sea that has made him so calm. All the same, behind the apparently smiling, boyish figure lurks a real Vestland devil, with inner strength, like the granite at the mouth of the fjord that stands firm against every onslaught.

Good luck with the book and in the future. Now the fun will begin. Everything else was probably just a warm-up! I am full of admiration for what you have accomplished.

Eyvind Hellstrøm
Master Chef
July 2009

THE DREAM

The time had come. Paul Bocuse entered the arena. He walked slowly, like the seconds ticking away in time with Geir's heartbeats. He looked at the legendary Frenchman who was about to announce the winner. Norway. Would he say Norway?

A sea of flags waved above the stands. Right at the front stood the podium. Geir hardly dared think about standing on the top. Anything other than gold would be a loss for him. But had it really gone that well? The herb oil he forgot, the beef he didn't season properly. Suppose he were to lose? All those people who would be disappointed, the long way home, the dream he had had for so long, but maybe, just maybe …

Then Paul Bocuse went over to the microphone.

MAYBE JESUS LIKED CINNAMON BUNS?

A little fair-haired boy stood at the kitchen door. He had just come home from kindergarten and he could smell them out in the street – Mum's freshly-baked buns. They were cooling on a rack on the worktop. Geir looked at the finished buns in consternation and pouted. Then the tears began to fall. He had wanted to help with the baking!

It was better than football or anything – a lump of bun dough on the kitchen worktop. You could make so many different things out of dough. He liked making things. Building oil rigs from lego. Sewing patterns in pretty colours on a piece of embroidery. Building huts in the woods. Carving knives from wood at the boys' club in the meeting house.

He could see the meeting house from the kitchen window. It was white and had a kind of spire on the top. He was given juice and cinnamon buns there every Sunday. Maybe Jesus liked cinnamon buns? Geir certainly did. But he didn't like to think that all those people who didn't believe in Jesus would burn in hell. But that was what the ladies at the meeting house said.

Geir thought it was bit silly that he had to be a Christian for the rest of his life because of what they said about hell. He'd rather be in the vegetable garden with his granddad than at the meeting house, because there were lots of nice-tasting things growing in the vegetable garden.

Rhubarb with sugar. Turnips and radishes. Chives that taste so good on marie biscuits. He discovered that taste for himself. He liked discovering new flavours. He also liked watching when Dad was standing in the kitchen cutting up whole lambs and half pigs that had come straight from the slaughterhouse. Then he plied his father with so many questions that his head would start to spin. "Why do you do it like that, Dad?"

He went on asking the same question. Asking teachers and chefs, anyone who has something to teach.

"Why do you do it like that?"

"I baked lots of buns when I was little, mainly because I thought it was so exciting to watch the dough change."

In the cookery room at Fitjar school. Here, Geir is with his former home economics teacher, Gerd Myrmel Træet. – I'm very proud to have taught a real world champion, says Gerd with a smile.

CINNAMON WHIRLS

Makes about 30

200 g/7 oz butter
700 ml/ milk
1 packet dried yeast (preferably the kind for sweet dough,
as it's a bit stronger)
170 g/6 oz sugar
1 tsp cardamom
Approx. 1 kg/2 lb 4 oz plain flour
1 egg for brushing

For the filling:
200 g/7 oz butter
100 g/3½ oz sugar
cinnamon

You can also put raisins and chopped nuts in the buns.

Melt the butter, pour in the milk and heat to body temperature.
Transfer to the mixer bowl and add the flour, cardamom, sugar
and dried yeast. Knead to a dough at medium speed for
10 minutes. If the dough is very sticky, add a little more flour.
Set aside to rise in a warm place until the dough has doubled in
size. Remove from the bowl and roll on a floured surface to a
thickness of 5 mm/¼ inch. Cut shavings of butter with a cheese
slice and lay them on the dough. Sprinkle over a good layer of
sugar and then with cinnamon. Roll the dough into a sausage
shape and cut in slices 3–4 cm/1¼–1½ ins thick. Arrange on a
baking sheet lined with baking parchment. When all the slices
have been placed on the baking sheet, cover with a cloth and set
aside again to rise in a warm place. The buns are ready for baking
when they have at least doubled in size. It is important that they
rise sufficiently so they will be nice and light. Brush with a little
beaten egg and bake for 15 minutes at 180 °C/350°F. Leave to cool on
a wire rack (but they are best when warm, straight from the
oven!).

Moister cinnamon buns

Shave cold butter onto the dough with a
cheese slice. This will give you a thicker layer
of butter and the buns will be moister.

3 KINDS ᴼꜰ MUFFINS

150 g/5½ oz dairy butter
150 g/5½ oz sugar
2 eggs
1 tsp baking powder
175 g/6 oz plain flour
170 g/6 oz fresh berries, chocolate, nuts or fruit of your choice

For this recipe it is important that all the ingredients should be at the same temperature, otherwise the mixture may easily split.

Cream the butter and sugar together lightly. Beat in the eggs, one at a time. Mix in the baking powder, flour and most of the berries/fruit/chocolate/nuts.

Spoon the mixture into muffin tins and, if desired, put some berries/fruit/chocolate/nuts on top.

Bake the muffins at 170 °C/325 °F for 12–15 minutes (depending on the size of the tins). A handy way to check if they are ready is to stick a thin skewer or knitting needle into the muffins. If any mixture sticks to them, they are not ready and need to bake a little longer.

Leave to cool on a wire rack.

My versions here are one with cinnamon and pieces of apple, one with blackcurrants and chocolate and one with grated lemon peel (for this you only need the peel of ⅓ lemon for this recipe).

The muffins can be decorated with icing, which you make by putting icing sugar in a cup and gradually adding water (lemon juice is also good instead of water) until it has a thick consistency and can be spread on the muffins.

Check with a knitting needle

When you bake the muffins, you can check if they are ready by sticking a skewer or a knitting needle in them. If dough sticks to it, you have to bake them a little longer.

2 KINDS OF SPONGE ROLL

STRAWBERRY SPONGE ROLL

3 eggs
120 g/4 ¼ oz plain flour
1 tsp baking powder
250 g/9 oz sugar
A little extra sugar for sprinkling
250 g/9 oz strawberry jam
(use any strawberry jam you like)

Beat together the eggs and sugar. It is better to beat at low speed for a longer time than at high speed for a short time, because the mixture will be firmer and give a lighter, moister cake. Sift in the flour and baking powder and mix with a spatula. Spread the mixture over a baking sheet lined with baking parchment and bake for 8 minutes at 180 °C/350 °F. Remove from the oven and turn out onto a sheet of baking parchment or a cloth sprinkled with sugar. Leave to cool for 5 minutes before removing the baking parchment and spreading with jam as illustrated. Roll up the cake as tightly as you can without squeezing out all the jam. To serve, cut in slices.

CHOCOLATE SPONGE ROLL WITH BUTTERCREAM

3 eggs
1 egg white
125 g/4½ oz sugar
60 g/2 oz potato flour
2 tbsp cocoa
1 tsp baking powder

FOR THE BUTTERCREAM:
150 g/5½ oz butter, at room temperature
180 g/6 oz icing sugar
1 egg yolk

Beat the eggs, egg white and sugar to an airy mixture. Reserve the egg yolk to use in the buttercream. Mix the potato flour, cocoa and baking powder and sift over the egg and sugar mixture. Mix in with a spatula. Pour the mixture into the oven tray and spread out evenly. Bake for 8 minutes at 180 °C/350 °F. When it is ready, turn out as for the strawberry roll, but in this case allow to cool completely, covered with baking parchment or perhaps with the oven tray so it doesn't dry out. Make the buttercream while you wait for the sponge to cool.

BUTTERCREAM:
Beat the butter and icing sugar until white and then beat in the egg yolk. When the sponge has cooled, spread the buttercream over it and roll up as for the strawberry roll.

HOW TO MAKE SPONGE ROLL:

1. Spread the mixture over a baking sheet lined with baking parchment. Bake the sponge base.

2. Lay a fresh sheet of baking parchment on the worktop and sprinkle with sugar. Turn the baked sponge out onto the fresh sheet of paper. (This is easy as long the cake sticks to the baking parchment.) Carefully remove the upper sheet of baking parchment. Spread with the jam.

3. Use the baking parchment to roll up the cake. Roll quite tightly, especially to start with.

4. Finally remove the baking parchment again and press the sponge roll together well.

Geir at his mother's childhood home on Fitjar, where he spent a lot of time as a child.

In the kitchen of the house on Fitjar. Geir is helping his father Arve with Sunday dinner – roast pork with sauerkraut and gravy.

"Granny told me you can't eat rhubarb after Midsummer's Day, because it gets woody."

RHUBARB COMPOTE WITH CREAM AND MILK

RHUBARB COMPOTE:
1 kg/2 lb 4 oz rhubarb
200 g/7 oz sugar
50 ml/3 tbsp water
1 tbsp potato flour
1 tbsp water

CREAM AND MILK:
100 ml/3½ fl oz cream
100 ml/3½ fl oz whole milk

RHUBARB COMPOTE:
Wash the rhubarb thoroughly. Cut off the leaves and the bottom 5 cm/2 ins of the stalk (the slightly flatter part). Cut into 2 cm/¾ inch pieces and put in a saucepan with the sugar and 50 ml/3 tablespoons water. Cover, bring to the boil and cook for 5 minutes. It should be cooked through and starting to fall apart. Mix together the potato flour and 1 tablespoon water and pour into the rhubarb, stirring continuously. It shouldn't boil for more than 10 seconds after the compote thickens. Set aside to cool in individual portions or in a large bowl.

CREAM AND MILK:
Eat the rhubarb compote cold with a mixture of cream and milk, and a little sugar.

To make it a bit more exciting, you can top it with fresh strawberries when serving. You can also make basil-flavoured milk (which is delicious with strawberries and rhubarb). Just whiz 10 basil leaves in a blender with the milk (before mixing it with the cream) until it is completely green, then mix in the cream and serve with the rhubarb.

Vary it with strawberries

Strawberries taste delicious in combination with rhubarb, so you can put strawberries in the compote as well. You can also vary the flavour with cinnamon and/or vanilla.

"LAPPER" WITH CRUSHED RASPBERRIES

"LAPPER":
2 eggs
500 ml/18 fl oz sour milk
2 tsp baking soda
150 g/5 oz flour
100 g/3½ oz sugar

CRUSHED RASPBERRIES:
300 g/10½ oz raspberries
(frozen or fresh – we often did this at Granny's after picking raspberries in the garden).
3 tbsp sugar

"LAPPER":
Pour the milk into a bowl, beat in the flour and sugar and lastly the eggs. Leave the batter to stand for 30 minutes for the flour to swell (dissolve properly in the mixture so it absorbs liquid). Then mix in the baking soda. Heat a frying-pan to medium heat and add a little butter. With a small ladle, pour in sufficient batter to give a pancake of the size you want. I often make 10 cm/4 inch pancakes, but they can be smaller or larger if you like. When the pancake begins to cook through, turn it and finish cooking. Place on a wire rack and eat immediately – or make a batch and eat them afterwards. They are best when freshly made!

CRUSHED RASPBERRIES:
Stir the raspberries and sugar together with a fork to crush the berries. The raspberries may vary a little in sweetness, so you should taste them to check if more sugar is needed.

Let the batter rise

It's a good idea to make the batter half an hour in advance, so it can rise. Then mix in the baking soda just before you start cooking.

"Eating lapper was like having cakes on weekdays, and they were fantastic with raspberries from Granny's garden."

CHOUX BUNS WITH VANILLA CREAM

CHOUX PASTRY:
100 g/3½ oz butter
250 ml/8½ fl oz water
150 g/5½ oz plain flour
4 eggs

VANILLA CREAM:
1 vanilla pod
400 ml/14 fl oz milk
6 egg yolks
40 g/1½ oz sugar
1 tbsp cornflour
200 ml/7 fl oz cream, whipped stiff

CHOUX PASTRY:

Cut the butter in pieces and bring to the boil with the water. Add all the flour and stir well until it forms a smooth ball. Remove from the heat when the dough comes away from the pan. Add the eggs one by one, stirring well in between. The mixture should be firm enough not to run. Using two spoons, arrange knobs of dough on baking sheets. Leave a good distance in between, so the buns don't run together. They will double or treble in size during baking. Bake for 25 minutes at 200 °C/400 °F. Leave to cool on a wire rack.

VANILLA CREAM:

Split the vanilla pod lengthways and scrape out the seeds. Bring the milk, vanilla and sugar to the boil.

Mix the egg yolks with the cornflour. Gradually pour a little of the hot milk mixture over the egg yolks, stirring continuously. Pour the mixture back into the saucepan and simmer gently until it thickens. Allow to cool completely and fold in the whipped cream.

HOW TO MAKE CHOUX PASTRY:

1. In a saucepan, bring butter and water to the boil. Add flour.

2. Beat well over medium heat until the choux dough comes away from the pan. After about 5 minutes you will have a nice firm dough. It should look like it does in the picture.

3. Beat in the eggs one at a time.

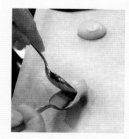

4. Using a dessert spoon, arrange balls of dough about the size of an egg on baking parchment.

FISH BALLS IN CURRY SAUCE

800 g/1 lb 12 oz fish balls, bought or home made
(see recipe for fish cake mix on page 38, herring fishcakes)

FOR THE SAUCE:
500 ml/18 fl oz stock from the fish balls
70 g/2¾ oz butter
70 g/2¾ oz plain flour
2 tbsp curry powder
500 ml/18 fl oz milk
200 g /7 oz peeled prawns

VEGETABLES:
2 carrots, thinly sliced
½ cauliflower, in florets
10 cm/4 ins leek, thinly sliced

Salt, black pepper and lemon juice

Heat the milk and fish stock in a saucepan. In another pan, melt the butter and fry the curry in the butter for 30 seconds to bring out the flavour. Add the flour and stir thoroughly. Gradually add hot stock/milk, stirring continuously so the sauce does not go lumpy. You are more likely to get lumps if you add cold liquid directly to the flour mixture. That's why we use hot stock.

Add the carrots and let the sauce simmer for 5 minutes before adding the remaining vegetables and the fish balls. Cook for a further 5 minutes. Season the sauce with salt and pepper, and perhaps a little lemon juice. Add the prawns and serve!

To make the sauce more interesting, you can add 1 stalk lemon grass, ¼ red chilli, 2 lime leaves, 1 teaspoon coriander seeds, 1 whole cardamom and the zest of one lime when you fry the curry. You can also use coconut milk instead of milk. When everything is ready, flavour with lime juice. This gives it a slightly more interesting and exotic taste, which I prefer!

HOW TO MAKE WHITE SAUCE (BÉCHAMEL SAUCE)

1. Melt the butter.

2. Stir in the flour. Remove the pan from the heat.

3. Heat the milk in a separate pan. Gradually add the milk to the roux, stirring continuously.

4. Simmer for 10 minutes.

COULD HE BECOME THE WORLD'S BEST CHEF?

– "Who's that guy?" Geir was watching the chef on television appearing with Ingrid Espelid Hovig. He had been a bit late switching on the television – they'd had to do a few extra sprints at the end of football practice that day, and then he had to make himself a sandwich, because he was hungry. Usually he always made it back in time for the television cookery programme.

He was 13 years old and he often made Ingrid Espelid's recipes for dinner. He made lots of other things as well. Like the caramel (fudge) he tried to bake in the microwave just before Christmas. Suddenly great clouds of black smoke came billowing out of the microwave, so he had to open the window, and of course the black smoke billowed out of the window as well. Luckily none of the neighbours rang the fire brigade, but Mum had to do all the Christmas cleaning all over again. She was a bit cross.

If football practice had gone on even longer that day, maybe the moment that was to shape his future would never have arrived. Maybe there would have been a different kind of moment, a different sort of dream that would have ended in his becoming a doctor or something similar, as he was very good at maths and chemistry at school. "You ought to be more than just a cook," said his maths teacher a few years later, when Geir wanted to go to domestic science college. But by then it was too late.

That's because the man on the television was Bent Stiansen, and Ingrid Espelid's voice sounded even more excited than usual when she introduced him, explaining that Stiansen had just won the Bocuse d'Or, the WORLD CHAMPIONSHIP of cooking.

Geir almost choked on his sandwich. He had realised that he would not get to be a professional footballer, but he was bubbling over with excitement in the belief that absolutely anything else was possible. Could he become the world's best chef?

THAT was what he wanted to be!

AGED 10-16

"I learned a huge amount from Ingrid Espelid Hovig's food programmes, but I couldn't cheat like she did."

BAKED FISH
WITH PEPPERS AND LEEKS

800 g/1 lb 12 oz fillets of white fish
such as cod, haddock, pollock, coley
1 red pepper
1 leek
100 g/3½ oz butter
1 lemon
2 tsp salt
a little pepper

Cut the fish into 100 g/3½ oz pieces and place in a greased
ovenproof dish. Cut the pepper and leek in thin slices and lay
them on top together with knobs of butter. Squeeze over the
juice of 1 lemon. Season with salt and pepper. Cover the dish
with aluminium foil and bake in the oven for 15 minutes
at 180 °C/350 °F. You can check if the fish is ready by sticking
a fork in it to see if it is white and not shiny inside. Serve with
the stock from the dish and boiled potatoes.

This is a dish I often made in the microwave. That was the time
when we got our first microwave at home. If you do it in the
microwave, you must put it in a baking dish made of plastic, glass
or porcelain with a tight-fitting lid, or covered with plastic film.
You can't use aluminium foil in the microwave! Cooking time
approx. 6–8 minutes on full power in the microwave, depending
on the type of microwave oven.

Vary it with any kind of white fish

You can use any kind of white fish for this dish, such as
coley, monkfish, cod and pollock.

HERRING FISHCAKES

HERRING FISHCAKES:
1 kg/2 lb 4 oz herring fillets (the skin can be retained as long as the scales are removed)
3 eggs
300 ml/10 fl oz whole milk
18 g/¼ oz salt
black pepper
You can also add 1 sprig of parsley and the grated zest of 1 lemon, if desired

BROWNED ONIONS:
2 yellow onions
100 g/3½ oz butter
salt

SUMMER CABBAGE STEAMED IN BUTTER:
1 summer cabbage/spring cabbage
3 tbsp butter
1 tsp salt
50 ml/2 fl oz water

200 ml/7 fl oz sour cream
boiled potatoes

HERRING FISHCAKES:
When making fishcake mixtures, it is very important that everything should be ice cold, both the ingredients and the equipment. You could put the food processor bowl in the freezer for 10 minutes before using it. Put the herring fillets in the food processor and blend for 2 minutes. Add salt and blend for a further minute. Add the eggs, and the parsley and grated lemon zest if desired, and mix well. Add the milk in a thin stream. Form the mixture into cakes using a moistened spoon and your hand. Fry in a pan with a little butter over medium heat. I fry them in the pan until golden, then transfer them all to a baking sheet and finish by baking them in the oven at 180 °C/350 °F for about 5 minutes. That makes it a bit quicker.

BROWNED ONIONS:
Cut the onion in strips. Put in a pan with the butter. Fry over low heat for about 20 minutes. The onion should be tender and golden brown. Season with salt and pepper.

This is a general recipe for all fishcake mixtures. Instead of herring you can use coley, pollock, haddock, catfish or salmon. The cakes may be boiled as fish balls if you don't like fried food.

SUMMER CABBAGE STEAMED IN BUTTER:
Cut the cabbage into 8 large wedges, keeping the stalk attached so it won't fall apart. Put in a saucepan with water in the bottom. Sprinkle with a little salt and spread the butter on top. Cover and cook over full heat. From the time it begins to steam until it is ready takes 3–4 minutes. It should be just al dente.

HOW TO MAKE FISHCAKES:

1. Grind the fish in a food processor until it is roughly chopped.

2. Add salt and pepper. Grind again. Add the eggs. Blend until the mixture is smooth.

3. Add milk – a little at a time.

4. Add grated lemon zest.

5. Form the mixture into balls in your hand with a dessert spoon. Use the spoon to press the cakes flatter in the pan before frying them.

"I always put curly leaf parsley on potatoes, because that's what Ingrid Espelid did."

"This is a typical Norwegian pizza with plenty of dough, topping and cheese."

SATURDAY PIZZA WITH PIZZA SALAD

DOUGH:
300 ml/10 fl oz water, at body
temperature
500 g/1 lb 2 oz plain flour
2 tbsp olive oil
1 tsp salt
½ packet yeast (dried or fresh)

DOUGH:

Put the water and olive oil in the mixer
bowl and dissolve the fresh yeast in it
(if using fresh yeast). Add the flour and
salt and the dried yeast (if using dried
yeast), and knead at medium speed for
10 minutes with the dough hook. If the
dough is not firm enough, add a little
more flour. Cover the bowl with a cloth
and set aside to rise while you make the
topping.

TOPPING:
450 g/1 lb minced meat
1 yellow onion, roughly chopped
1 garlic clove, finely chopped
(may be omitted)
200 g/7 oz mushrooms
1 tin tomatoes
2 tbsp tomato purée
100 ml/3½ fl oz water
1 tbsp plain flour
salt and pepper, and a little oregano or
thyme, if desired
300 g/10½ oz grated cheese, if possible
mozzarella, which is the original
semi-hard pizza cheese

TOPPING:

Fry the minced meat in a casserole with the
onion and garlic. Add the tomato purée and
the tinned tomatoes and simmer gently. Mix
the flour and water and add to the pan. If
you want to add a little oregano or thyme,
chop finely and add now. These are herbs
that need to be cooked to bring out the
flavour. Cook for 10 minutes. Season with
salt and pepper. Set aside to cool (to a
maximum of 37 °C/98 °F) before spreading it
on the pizza dough. (If the topping is hot
when you spread it on the dough, the yeast
will die and the pizza dough will not rise.)

With a rolling pin, roll out the pizza dough
on a floured surface. Line a baking sheet
with baking parchment and transfer the
dough to the baking sheet. Pull the dough
gently so it covers the whole of the baking
sheet. Spoon over the topping and leave the
pizza to rise to double its height. Sprinkle
with the cheese. Bake for 20 minutes
at 200 °C/400 °F.

PIZZA SALAD:
½ cabbage
4 tbsp vinegar (7% acidity)
1 tbsp sugar
1 tsp salt
2 tbsp neutral oil

PIZZA SALAD:

It's a good idea to make the salad first,
because it's fine to let it stand for a while.
Shred the cabbage. Mix all the other
ingredients in a bowl, pour over the
cabbage and mix well. Cover with a lid or
plastic film and refrigerate until it's time
to serve.

Chill the topping

Remember to chill the topping a
little before spreading it on the
dough, otherwise the dough
will be spoiled.

Pizza salad was not a part of my
childhood but it's something I
always have with pizza at home
now. I tasted it for the first time
about 10 years ago in Sweden. All
the pizza restaurants in Sweden
serve it with pizza, and you often
get a bowl of pizza salad on the
table as an appetiser, before you
get the pizza. This bowl then goes
on the next table when you've
finished with it.

"I have deep roots in Hardanger; my father comes from there. When I was little, we often went there to pick fruit. Hardanger is one of the finest places I know in Norway."

Tinned beans

This casserole can be made with different types of beans. It's a good idea to buy tinned beans, because they're ready to use and don't need to be soaked.

COWBOY CASSEROLE

CASSEROLE:
450 g/1 lb minced meat
200 g/7 oz bacon
1 yellow onion, roughly chopped
2 tbsp tomato purée
1 tin baked beans
1 tin chilli beans
2 tbsp plain flour
200 ml/7 fl oz water
tabasco and salt

CREAMED POTATO:
1 kg/2 lb 4 oz floury potatoes, such as Kerr's Pink or almond potatoes
200 ml/7 fl oz whole milk
3 tbsp butter
salt and black pepper

CASSEROLE:

In a large frying pan, fry the mince and the diced bacon in a little oil over high heat. Add the onion and fry until transparent. Add tomato purée and fry briefly to get rid of the raw taste. Add the beans. Put the flour and water in a jar with a lid and shake to mix and get rid of any lumps. Pour into the casserole. Cook for 10 minutes. Flavour with salt and tabasco sauce. I like it rather hot, so I use quite a lot of tabasco!

CREAMED POTATO:

Peel the potatoes and put in a saucepan with sufficient water to cover them. Cover and boil until soft. It is best not to heat the water to a rolling boil, otherwise the potatoes will fall apart. Use a knife to check when the potatoes are soft. It should pass easily through the potato. Pour off the water and mash the potatoes with a potato masher or a strong whisk. Add the milk and butter and season with salt and pepper. If the mashed potato is too thick, add more milk.

It's a good idea to start by putting the potatoes on to boil, as they take the longest time.

HOW TO MAKE CREAMED POTATO:

1. Use floury potatoes, such as almond potatoes. Bring to the boil and leave the potatoes to simmer over medium heat until soft. Pour off the water and put the pan of potatoes back on the hob until any remaining water has completely evaporated. Squeeze the potatoes through a sieve.

2. Gradually stir the milk into the mashed potatoes. It is important to use warm milk!

3. Add the butter at the same time as you stir in the milk.

SPAGHETTI BOLOGNESE

Make the meat sauce in the same way as for the pizza topping on page 41.

400 g/14 oz spaghetti
3 litres/5¼ pints water
6 tsp salt
4 tbsp good quality olive oil

Bring the salted water to the boil in a large saucepan. When it boils, tip in the spaghetti, stirring gently so it separates in the pan and doesn't just form a large lump. Cook without the lid. The cooking time varies from one brand to another. Check the packet and sample the spaghetti just before it is supposed to be ready. It is best when just cooked through. Drain in a large strainer and mix with the olive oil. This will prevent it from forming lumps.

When buying good quality olive oil, it is best to check the date. It should be as fresh as possible, and definitely not produced more than one year ago. Keep the oil in the refrigerator, otherwise it will go rancid.

HOW TO CUT ONIONS:

1. Start by cutting in towards the root of the onion, but stop when you get to the root. The slices should remain attached to the onion.

2. Then turn the onion round and cut in the opposite direction and, hey presto, you have a chopped onion!

Check the consistency of the pasta!

Bring the water to the boil before you put in the spaghetti, otherwise the strands will stick together. It's quite a good idea to add a little cooking oil to the water. Take care not to cook pasta for too long, otherwise it will go soft and lose its proper consistency.

CRÈME CARAMEL

300 ml/10 oz cream
700 ml/1¼ pints whole milk
7 eggs
250 g/9 oz sugar
½ vanilla pod
100 g/3½ oz sugar for the caramel

Scrape the seeds out of the vanilla pod. Bring the cream, milk, vanilla pod and seeds, and 250 g/9 oz sugar to the boil. Set aside on the worktop for 30 minutes to draw out the flavour of the vanilla.

Meanwhile, make the caramel to put in the bottom of the moulds or heat-resistant glasses. Put 100 g/3½ oz sugar in a small saucepan over medium heat. When it begins to melt, stir gently to prevent the sugar from burning, but do not stir too much or it will crystallise. When all the sugar has caramellised, pour it directly into the mould(s) you are going to use.

Whisk the eggs and stir in the milk mixture. Strain into the moulds.

Bake in a bain-marie at 100 °C/210 °F until it has set. To test whether it has set, shake the mould gently. The cream should be firm. You can also test by inserting a knife. if only caramel sticks to it, it is ready. It takes about 30 minutes in small moulds and 90 minutes in a large loaf tin.

You can bake this in any kind of mould. It is baked at only 100 °C/210 °F, which most glass, and porcelain can withstand, but don't use your best crystal glasses!

I made chocolate spirals for decoration. You make these by melting dark chocolate and piping it onto baking parchment as shown below. Refrigerate until serving.

TO MAKE CHOCOLATE SPIRALS:

1. Spoon the chocolate mixture into a piping bag. Pipe random spiral patterns on a sheet of baking parchment.

2. Set aside to cool. When cool, carefully remove the chocolate decorations from the parchment.

3. Decorate the dessert with the chocolate.

SPICY MARBLE CAKE

CAKE:
125 g/4 oz butter
275 g/9¾ oz sugar
2 eggs, not separated
250 g/9 oz plain flour, sieved
2 tsp baking powder
1 tsp ground nutmeg
1 tsp ground cinnamon
250 ml/8½ fl oz whole milk
3 tbsp cocoa powder

ICING:
45 g/1¾ oz butter, at room temperature
300 g/10½ oz icing sugar
2 tbsp cocoa powder
4 tbsp coffee (preferably espresso)
50 ml/2 fl oz milk for moistening

CAKE:

Grease a 24 cm/9½ inch round springform cake tin with butter. Put in a little flour and shake to cover the tin. Cream together the butter and sugar, and mix in the eggs one at a time. Sift in the flour, baking powder, nutmeg and cinnamon alternately with the milk. Lastly, divide the mixture in two and add the cocoa to one portion. Spoon the pale mixture into the bottom of the cake tin and the dark mixture on top. Stir gently with a fork to give a marbled effect. Bake at 160 °C/320 °F for 45 minutes. Test with a skewer to see if it is done. Remove the cake from the tin cover with a cloth, and leave to cool on a wire rack. It's a good idea to turn it upside down, because that way it is more likely to be smooth and level on top.

ICING:

To make the icing, mix all the ingredients together. When the cake has cooled, cut it in two horizontally. Moisten the inner surfaces of the cake with milk. Spread 1/3 of the icing on the bottom layer. Put on the top layer and spread the remaining icing over the top and sides of the cake with a spatula. Make a decorative pattern on the top with a fork.

Set aside for two days

It's a good idea to set this cake aside for two days before eating, as this will make it moister and bring out the flavour.

"This was my favourite cake when
I was little, and I only had it at
my granny's in Hardanger."

THE ART OF MAKING KOMLER IN A HOWLING GALE

He may have been born with the salt spray in his hair, on an island in the middle of a scattered group of islets at the edge of the ocean, but his father's home-built boat kept to the landward side of the skerries. Geir and his little brother went diving for crabs and mussels, which they roasted on open fires. When Geir got a job as a cook on a fishing boat, it didn't keep inside the skerries. The trouble started just outside Egersund, and soon the sea turned into a roller-coaster ride without a stop button.

Geir was 17 and studying at the domestic science college on Fitjar. He was spared having to learn "the art of serving your husband home-made cakes when he wakes up from his midday nap" and other such important things, but he learned a lot about making good, Norwegian food like komler. But he had never made komler in a gale force wind.

It didn't come to that either, because the ship's cook's had gone bright green in the face and he felt as if he was about to die. The fishing boat was old and sat badly in the water. It bobbed up and down all the time, and even worse, it smelt of herrings – old stale herrings – down below and that doesn't do anything for seasickness.

He wished he had never done it. Never again would he allow himself to be tempted to earn a fast buck by going to sea. Why hadn't he just stayed working in the kitchen at Fitjar Fjordhotell, where he had a great job while he went through college – even if he had to make mushroom soup using the juice from the can as stock and roast pork with frozen mixed vegetables from a catering pack. A dash of Aromat (a flavour enhancer), and everything was fine... Even the frozen steak he put in the microwave and cooked until it was grey all through; after all, it had to be defrosted. The guests didn't generally get angry.

But hungry fishermen can get very angry. The catch was bad, and on top of that the crew had to make their own food, because far out in the fishing grounds somewhere between Norway and England Geir was lying in his cabin immediately above the propeller. It made even more noise than the sea, and he had no thoughts to spare for the dream of winning the Bocuse d'Or.

All he dreamt of was getting ashore again.

"The sea has always been important for me. Right from when I was a little boy, I found food in the sea: sea urchins, fish, mussels and other shellfish."

"KOMLER"
– POTATO DUMPLINGS

"KOMLER":
800 g/1 lb 12 oz peeled potatoes
salt and pepper
120 g/4 ¼ oz (approx.) barley meal
2 smoked pork knuckles
1 swede, roughly chopped
4 carrots, roughly chopped
1 vossakorv sausage

"GARNISH":
200 g/7 oz bacon, cut in pieces
1 tbsp butter

"KOMLER":
Boil the pork knuckles for 2½ hours. Grate the potatoes or put them through a mincer. Sprinkle with salt and mix in the barley meal. The mixture mustn't be so runny that the potato dumplings go mushy, nor so firm that they get heavy. Make round balls of mixture with your hands, put in the water with the pork knuckles and simmer for 40 minutes.

After 30 minutes, add the chopped carrots and swede.

After a further 10 minutes, add the sausage

GARNISH:
Fry the bacon in butter until crisp.

"This is my version of komler. There are a great many ways of making them and different accompaniments. On Fitjar they use salted lamb instead of pork knuckle and sausage. But my version is partly due to the fact that my father is from Hardanger, hence the smoked meat and vossakorv sausage."

PRAWN COCKTAIL

½ iceberg lettuce
½ cucumber, peeled
300 g/10½ oz prawns, peeled
½ lemon
1 sprig dill
½ red pepper
1 stick celery

THOUSAND ISLAND DRESSING:
100 g/3½ oz mayonnaise
1 tbsp ketchup
2 tbsp pickled gherkins, finely chopped
1 tbsp red pepper, finely chopped
4 drops Worcester sauce
2 drops tabasco
1 hard boiled egg, finely chopped

Mix all the ingredients for the thousand island dressing in a bowl and refrigerate.

Wash the lettuce and tear in smallish pieces. Cut the cucumber in sticks or cubes. Cut the celery and the pepper in thin slices. Put all the ingredients in layers in a cocktail glass, with a little dressing in between each layer. Top with a little extra dressing, a lemon wedge and a little dill. Serve with nice bread.

You can vary the ingredients a little. I also think it's nice with a little avocado and mango/papaya in the salad. With a little coriander and chilli sauce in the dressing as well it's really good.

COLEY STEAKS WITH ONION

COLEY STEAKS:
800 g/1 lb 12 oz coley fillets from the back
2 tbsp whole wheat meal
or coarse rye meal
salt and black pepper
1 tbsp neutral oil
2 tbsp butter

CREAMED VEGETABLES:
1 onion
1 carrot
½ swede
½ celeriac
2 tbsp butter
salt and pepper

ONIONS AND POTATOES:
2 onions
2 tbsp butter
800 g/1 lb 2 oz new
or thin-skinned potatoes
3 tbsp capers
4 soft boiled eggs
1 lemon

COLEY STEAKS:
Salt the fish before frying, preferably a few hours beforehand. Dip the skin side in a little flour and fry the fish on the skin side in neutral oil until golden. Transfer to a baking sheet with the butter and bake for about 8 minutes at 150 °C/300 °F.

CREAMED VEGETABLES:
Peel all the vegetables and boil in a little water until tender. Use as little water as possible, as it takes away the nice flavour. Pour off the water and dry the vegetables well. Purée in a blender with the butter to a smooth cream and season with salt and pepper.

ONION AND POTATOES:
Boil the potatoes in their skins until done. Cut in chunks. Sauté the onion in butter until soft and golden. Add the capers and potatoes. Season with salt, lemon juice and pepper. Serve with segments of warm, soft-boiled egg.

HOW TO COAT FISH:

1. Salt the fish the day before, so it goes firm. Place the fish steaks skin side down in coarse rye meal.

2. I only coat the skin side, as in this recipe, but you can coat them all over.

"BIFFSNADDER" – STRIPS ᵒꜰ STEAK

"BIFFSNADDER":
800 g/1 lb 4 oz steak, in strips, (preferably sirloin or rump)
200 g/7 oz mushrooms
1 head broccoli
1 small tin sweetcorn (may be omitted)
1 red pepper
1 yellow onion
200 ml 7 fl oz cream
salt and black pepper
oil for frying

POTATO WEDGES:
1 kg/2 lb 4 oz almond potatoes
or other good potatoes
4 cloves garlic
1 sprig rosemary
100 ml/3½ fl oz good quality olive oil
2 tbsp butter
salt and black pepper
½ lemon, sliced

SALAD:
½ red curly lettuce
1 little gem lettuce
½ cucumber
4 tomatoes
2 tbsp good quality olive oil
2 tbsp lemon juice
salt and pepper

"BIFFSNADDER":
Cut up all the ingredients beforehand, as things go quickly once you start cooking. Split the broccoli into florets. Cut the onion, pepper and mushrooms in slices. Put a frying pan on high heat. When it starts to smoke, add the oil. Fry the strips of steak until well browned. Add the mushrooms, red pepper and onion and fry until the onion is transparent. Add the broccoli, sweetcorn and cream, reduce the heat to medium, cover and cook for 5 minutes. Season with salt and pepper. You could also add a little finely chopped tarragon to give a slight "béarnaise" flavour.

POTATO WEDGES:
Wash the potatoes thoroughly and cut in wedges. Put the wedges in an ovenproof dish and mix with all the other ingredients. Bake at 180 °C/350 °F for 40 minutes. The potatoes should be soft and golden. It's a good idea to turn the potatoes after 20 minutes so they don't get overcooked on top.

SALAD:
Wash the lettuce and dry thoroughly, preferably in a salad spinner. Slice the cucumber and tomatoes, add the lettuce and dress with lemon juice and olive oil. Season with salt and pepper. It is important to dress and season the salad just before serving. If you do it a long time in advance, the lettuce will go limp and nasty.

Brown over high heat

It is important to fry the meat over very high heat so that it browns well on the outside, otherwise it will cook.

ANOTHER GOOD DRESSING FOR SALAD:
Put 1 tbsp Dijon mustard in a bowl together with 1 tbsp red wine vinegar and stir in 100 ml/3½ fl oz good quality olive oil. You could also add 1 finely chopped shallot. Will keep for two weeks in the refrigerator in an airtight container.

NORWEGIAN LAMB STEW

2 kg/4½ lb stewing mutton or lamb
(preferably leg, because it is more meaty)
1 cabbage
2 tbsp whole black peppercorns
3 tbsp salt
4 tbsp plain flour
500 ml/18 fl oz water

Rinse the meat under cold running water. Cut the cabbage in
wedges with the stalk. Place the meat and cabbage in layers in
a large saucepan, starting with a layer of meat, then cabbage,
which you sprinkle with a little flour, salt and pepper. Then add
another layer of meat and continue in the same way until you have
used all the meat and cabbage, finishing with a layer of cabbage.
Add the water, cover and simmer. It should cook for about
3–4 hours. You can tell if it is ready by checking whether the
meat comes away from the bone. Serve with boiled potatoes.
This stew is as good, if not better, the next day, so you can make
it one day and just warm it up the next day.

The best way to boil potatoes!

"Anyone" can boil potatoes, so they say. But did you know that the potato water
should be only just boiling, so don't boil them on full heat. That's because they will
fall apart more quickly if you boil them too hard. It is also important to add a little
salt to the water.

"Ferries are an important part of life for people on Fitjar; the beautiful scenery comes as a bonus."

FLENSBURGER WITH HIPPEN

HIPPEN (thin, crisp biscuits):
40 g/1½ oz icing sugar
40 g/1½ oz flour
40 g/1½ oz egg whites
20 g/1¾ oz melted butter

FLENSBURGER (ice cream with warm berries and egg liqueur):
1 litre/1¾ pints good quality vanilla ice cream
400 g/14 oz blackberries (frozen or fresh) or cherries
2 tbsp sugar
100 ml/3½ fl oz egg liqueur
100 ml/3½ fl oz cream

HIPPEN:
Mix all the ingredients together. Pipe out (as shown below) on baking parchment in any shapes you like. Bake at 180 °C/350 °F for 2–3 minutes until golden. If you're quick, after you take the biscuits out of the oven, you can remove them from the baking parchment and lay them over something round, so they will be curved when they cool. It is important to work quickly, because they soon harden.

FLENSBURGER:
Heat the blackberries and sugar in a saucepan to release some of the juice. Put balls of ice cream in individual dishes (it's a good idea to put the dishes in the freezer for 10 minutes first, so the ice cream will not melt so quickly.) pour over the egg liqueur and add the hot blackberries. Top with lightly whipped cream, and hippen.

HOW TO MAKE DECORATIVE CRISPY BISCUITS/HIPPEN:

1. Mix together egg whites, icing sugar and flour. Spoon the mixture into a piping bag and pipe small shapes on a baking sheet lined with baking parchment. Bake in the oven for 2–3 minutes.

2. Carefully remove the biscuit shapes from the paper and use them to decorate the ice cream dessert.

"Flensburger was my favourite ice cream dessert when I was young, even though I wasn't old enough to drink egg liqueur."

CHARLOTTE ROYALE

1 strawberry sponge roll (see page 22)
Cut in slices. Line a bowl with plastic film and then with slices of
sponge roll, so that the inside of the bowl is completely covered.
Refrigerate.

RASPBERRY GELATINE MOUSSE:
4 gelatine leaves
4 eggs
60 g/1 oz sugar
200 ml/7 fl oz raspberry preserve (or puréed raspberries)
300 ml/10 fl oz cream

Soak the gelatine in cold water. Whip the cream lightly. It is
important not to beat it too stiff, because it will become too solid.
Beat together the eggs and sugar, preferably at low speed. If there
are any sugar crystals remaining in the egg mixture, continue
beating a little longer. Put the gelatine in a saucepan with the
raspberry purée and heat to melt the gelatine. Gradually stir the
egg mixture into the purée. Don't stir too much or too much air
will be squeezed out. Lastly, stir this into the cream. Pour the
mousse mixture into the cake-lined bowl and refrigerate for at
least 4 hours. Then turn the bowl upside down on a dish, and
remove the bowl and plastic film. Serve with freshly puréed
raspberries.

> You can vary this recipe with any
> flavours you like – strawberry,
> cherry, orange, apple...

HOW TO MAKE GELATINE MOUSSE:

1. Soak the gelatine leaves
in iced water for 5
minutes.

2. Beat eggs and sugar
together. The mixture is
ready when it's so firm
you can write in it.

3. Bring a saucepan of
water to the boil and
remove from the heat.
Add the softened gelatine
leaves. Pour into the egg
mixture.

4. Whip cream in a
different bowl, pour into
the egg mixture and fold
in gently with a spatula.
Pour the mousse into
moulds and chill for a few
hours.

YEAST DOUGHNUTS

Use the same dough as for cinnamon whirls (see page 17)

200 ml/7 fl oz firm jam of your choice
I used rhubarb, which is my favourite

1 egg for brushing

1 litre neutral oil for frying (sunflower, corn, soya)

Roll out the dough as for the cinnamon whirls, but a little thinner (3–4 mm/1/8 inch). Cut out rounds with a pastry-cutter or a glass. Brush half of the rounds with beaten egg. Put a spoonful of jam on the remaining rounds. It is important not to put in too much jam or it will run out at the sides of the doughnuts and then the halves won't stick together. Place an egged round on top of a round with jam (brushed half down) and press the sides together so the jam can't leak out. Cover the doughnuts with a cloth and set aside in a warm place to double in size. While they are rising, heat the oil to 150 °C/300 °F. It's a good idea to have a cooking thermometer or a deep-fryer.

When the doughnuts have finished rising, drop them in the oil. When they are golden on one side, turn them with a wooden spoon so they cook on the other side as well. They take 2–3 minutes on each side. Lay them on a cloth or paper and then in a bowl of sugar. Shake the doughnuts around in the bowl, so they get covered with sugar, and cinnamon too, if desired. Leave to cool on a wire rack.

HOW TO MAKE YEAST DOUGHNUTS:

1. Roll out the dough and cut out rounds with a pastry-cutter or a glass.

2. Brush with egg. Place spoonfuls of filling on the rounds.

3. Cover with another round and press the edges together carefully. Allow the dough to rise for half an hour. Check that the edges are still firmly closed before frying, pressing them together again if necessary.

4. Fry the doughnuts in sunflower oil until golden, turning part-way through.

"IT'S NOT EASY WORKING AT MC DONALDS!"

The apprentice examination in Stavanger. Geir had to make lunch with hamburger and chips. He cut the potatoes in neat strips while the oil in the pan got hotter and hotter. As he put the chips into the pan, the worst happened – the chips caught fire!

He had spent two years working as an apprentice, first at Finnegaardsstuene in Bergen and later at Jans Mat- og Vinhus in Stavanger. He started his apprenticeship by complaining to the chef at Finnegaardsstuene about the marzipan cake. Geir said it ought to be filled with apricot jam instead of raspberry, because that's what his mother did, so there. That was just before he got the whole cake thrown in his face. The chef had actually worked at a Michelin restaurant in France, so what could a young whippersnapper like Geir have to boast about?

"Maybe it isn't always such a good idea to say what I think," thought Geir, with a sudden attack of soul-searching. No doubt there were a few teachers on Fitjar who would have liked to see that time come sooner. High self-esteem has its irritating sides.

But he wasn't so big headed when the chips caught fire during the exam. (Incidentally, he had completely forgotten his chef's hat, and he lost marks for that as well) Suppose he failed? That would have been really embarrassing for him after working as an apprentice in two of the best restaurants in Western Norway. Fortunately he hadn't told anyone that he was planning to win the Bocuse d'Or. He managed to rescue the chips, but then came the next challenge: the hamburger.

"It is too raw inside," said the examiner. And that wasn't all. Geir had put the salad under the hamburger instead of on top. "It's not easy working at McDonalds," continued the examiner, but this time Geir didn't manage to hold his tongue. He replied that hamburgers are much better when they are raw inside, and that the salad can just as well be underneath. So there.

Many years later, a friend of Geir's spoke to the same examiner, who told him that no other apprentice had ever answered him back. Geir was the only one. In the apprentice exam, you could be awarded distinction, merit or pass.

Geir got "pass".

AGED 18–22

"I began diving while I was an apprentice. It was nice to get away from angry chefs. Underwater, you were in a completely different world, and what's more, I found lots of good ingredients ..."

Juicy in the middle

It is very easy to make your own hamburgers, and then you can freeze them. Don't cook them right through, let them remain a bit juicy in the middle.

HAMBURGER, EXAMINATION STYLE

HAMBURGER BUNS (makes 8):
300 ml/10 fl oz water
500 g/1 lb 2 oz plain flour
½ packet yeast
1 tsp salt

HAMBURGER:
800 g/1 lb 12 oz minced steak
2 tsp tarragon, finely chopped
1 tsp ground black pepper

BÉARNAISE DRESSING:
1 egg yolk
1 tbsp white wine vinegar
2 dl neutral oil
1 tbsp Dijon mustard
1 tsp salt
2 tbsp tarragon, finely chopped
4 tbsp gherkins or pickled cucumbers, finely chopped
2 tbsp chives, finely chopped

CHIPS:
800 g/1 lb 12 oz floury potatoes, such as Kerr's Pink or Dali
1 litre/1¾ pints neutral oil for frying
salt and pepper

GARNISH:
2 large tomatoes
2 whole pickled cucumbers
lettuce

HAMBURGER BUNS:
In a mixing bowl, mix lukewarm water with the flour, yeast and salt. Knead for 10 minutes, cover with a cloth and set aside to rise for 30 minutes. Form the dough into 8 buns and arrange on a baking sheet lined with baking parchment. Press the buns flat, cover with a cloth and leave to double in size. Bake at 180 °C/350 °F for 15 minutes. Leave to cool on a wire rack. The buns may be toasted before inserting the hamburgers.

BURGERS:
Mix the meat with the other ingredients and form into 4 large or 8 smaller burgers on a sheet of baking parchment. Grill or fry until pink in the middle. The large ones will take 3-4 minutes on each side and the small ones 1½–2 minutes.

Then it is important to put the salad on top of the burger and not underneath!

BEARNAISE DRESSING:
Beat together the egg yolk, mustard, salt and vinegar. Add all the oil. Add the remaining ingredients and, if desired, season with a little more salt and black pepper. May be kept in the refrigerator for up to two weeks.

CHIPS:
Cut the potatoes in thickish sticks. Heat the oil to 120 °C/250 °F and fry the potatoes for 8 minutes. Transfer to a wire rack and refrigerate. Turn up the heat to 150 °C/300 °F and fry the potatoes for 5 minutes. Transfer to a wire rack and refrigerate. Finally, turn the heat up to 190 °C/375 °F and fry the potatoes until crisp and golden. Season with salt and pepper and serve immediately.

TO DRINK
Beer or cola goes best with a good burger. If you want wine, you could choose an American Zinfandel with enough sweetness and alcohol content to complement the dressing and the fat from the chips.

PRAWN SOUP WITH FENNEL SALAD

SOUP:
500 g/1 lb 2 oz prawns (preferably raw, for the stock)
½ carrot, finely chopped
½ yellow onion, finely chopped
1 clove garlic, finely chopped
1 slice lemon
1 sprig parsley
200 ml/7 fl oz cream
2 tbsp tinned tomatoes

FENNEL SALAD
1 fennel bulb
1 lemon

SOUP:
Wash and peel the prawns, reserving the prawns for the salad.
Make shellfish stock by frying the shells in oil in a very hot
casserole. After 3 minutes add all the vegetables and the tomatoes.
Cook for a further 2 minutes. Add sufficient cold water to cover the
prawns. Bring to the boil and simmer for 20 minutes, then strain.
Reduce a little and add the cream. Season with salt and pepper.
Froth up before serving

FENNEL SALAD:
Cut the fennel in thin slices and mix with the prawns. Flavour with
a little good quality olive oil, lemon juice, salt and pepper. Put the
fennel salad in warm bowls and pour the soup over it.

The prawns can also be lightly fried in a very hot pan with a little
oil. Put the prawns in for 20 seconds, transfer to a tray and serve.
It is important not to fry the prawns any longer than that as,
if you do, they will often go soft.

WINE TIPS

The good thing about this recipe is the flavours in the soup
and the sweetness of the prawns with a touch of acidity
from the lemon. These go well with a Pinot Grigio from the
Alto Adige, a wine with notes of acid and herbs with
a coolness that matches the flavours of the dish well.

SNAILS WITH GARLIC AND PARSLEY

24 snails in shell
100 g/3½ oz butter
2 tbsp good quality olive oil
grated zest of ½ lemon
2 sprigs parsley
2 cloves garlic
2 baguettes

Bring the butter to room temperature and whiz in a small blender with the oil, parsley, zest of lemon and garlic to give a smooth green mass. Place the snails close together in an ovenproof dish with the openings of the shells uppermost. Press the butter down into each shell. Bake on the top shelf of the oven at 220 °C/425 °F for 5–6 minutes. They should be lightly browned on top. Serve with slices of toasted baguette.

WINE TIPS
This dish has strong flavours from the garlic and parsley, plus quite a lot of fat from the butter. Here I would recommend an Aligoté from Southern Burgundy, which is slightly rich with no hint of oak, yet plenty of acid and alcohol to tackle the butter.

"The first time I made this dish at Le Canard, the chef broke the plate because I had overcooked the duck liver."

Baked apples are easy to make and can be flavoured according to what they will be used for. Here I used curry, but for dessert you can use cinnamon instead. You can also use baked apples in a salad; they give it a nice, fresh taste.

WINE TIPS
Foie gras is a fatty dish that needs a little alcohol and acid to break down the fat. The combination of slight spiciness and sweetness means that a Gewürztraminer or a Riesling from Alsace with plenty of residual sweetness will go well with this dish. Another possibility is a Smaragd Riesling from Wachau in Austria, which has enough body to cope with it.

FRIED DUCK FOIE GRAS WITH CURRIED APPLES AND BRIOCHE

BRIOCHE:
300 ml/10 fl oz beaten egg
500 g/1 lb 2 oz plain flour
10 g/¼ oz salt
75 g/2¾ oz sugar
15 g/¼ oz fresh yeast
200 g/7 oz soft butter

CURRIED APPLES:
2 nice red apples (such as Aroma, Gravenstein, Summer Red)
½ tsp curry powder
1 tbsp butter
1 tsp sugar

HERB SALAD:
assorted mild salad herbs (chervil, dill, basil)
½ lemon
a little good quality olive oil

SHERRY SYRUP:
50 ml/2 fl oz sherry vinegar
40 g/1½ oz sugar

FRIED DUCK FOIE GRAS:
4 x 60 gram/2 oz slices of duck foie gras
salt and pepper

BRIOCHE:
Mix together all the ingredients except for the butter and knead in a food processor for 6 minutes at low speed, then for 20 minutes at high speed. Add the butter and continue kneading for 24 minutes on low and 2 minutes on high. It is important to keep to this timing, as that will give you a good brioche dough. Transfer the dough to a loaf tin, cover with a cloth and set aside in a warm place to double in size. Bake for 40 minutes at 170 °C/325 °F. If you have a cooking thermometer, a good tip is that all kinds of bread should have an internal temperature of 95 °C/200 °F when ready! Set aside to cool on a wire rack. Brioche can be sliced and frozen, so you can take out just what you need.

SHERRY SYRUP:
Boil up the sherry vinegar with the sugar and cool.

HERB SALAD:
Prepare the herbs, but wait to dress them with lemon juice, salt, pepper and olive oil until immediately before serving.

CURRIED APPLES:
Peel the apples and cut in 2 cm/¾ inch cubes. Put a frying pan over high heat. When it begins to smoke, add the apple cubes and sprinkle with sugar and curry. When they are slightly browned/ caramellised on one side, shake the pan so they brown on all sides. Finally add a little butter. Finished! The apples should still be nice and firm. Make this just before you fry the foie gras.

FRIED DUCK FOIE GRAS:
Heat a frying pan over high heat. When it begins to smoke, put in the foie gras. Reduce the heat a little and fry for about 1 minute until it is a nice dark brown colour. Turn and fry for 2 minutes on the other side. Now add cubes of brioche and fry with the foie gras.

Arrange the brioche, foie gras, apples and herb salad in the form of a salad with the sherry syrup and finish by pouring over a little of the pan juices.

This isn't a dish for slimmers. Brioche is a very rich bread with a lot of eggs and butter, and the duck liver is almost entirely fat. Basically goose liver is better for frying, as is doesn't release o much fat, but it has a slightly stronger taste. Goose liver is more expensive too. In addition, the technique of producing high quality duck liver is now so well-developed that it retains almost all of its fat when frying

"I often dived for scallops on Fitjar. They can usually be found on the sandy seabed at a depth of 10–15 metres."

Don't boil shellfish for too long!

Shellfish are often boiled for too long, so it's a good idea to do it yourself! The fishermen back home on Fitjar say you should boil lobsters and crabs for 30 minutes, the same time as for the potatoes. If you do, you can guarantee they'll be dry!

SHELLFISH PLATTER

BOILED LOBSTERS, CRABS AND LANGOUSTINES:
2 lobsters,
each 600–800 g/1 lb 2 oz–1 lb 8 oz.
8 large langoustines,
each about 150 g/5½ oz.
2 large crabs,
each 600–800 g/1 lb 2 oz–1 lb 8 oz.
1 onion
1 carrot
½ fennel bulb
½ orange
1 tbsp coriander seeds
1 tbsp fennel seeds
salt
5 litres/8¾ pints water

OTHER SHELLFISH:
1.5 kg/3 lb 5 oz prawns
8 oysters
4 scallops

GARNISH:
1 lime
salt flakes
50 ml/2 fl oz red wine vinegar
1 shallot
2 lemons

BOILED SHELLFISH:
Peel and roughly chop the vegetables. Put in a saucepan of water with all the herbs and boil for 10 minutes. Add sufficient salt for the water to taste like sea water – about 3 tablespoons per litre. Bring back to the boil and add the crabs. Continue to boil. After 5 minutes add the lobsters and continue boiling. After a further 5 minutes add the langoustines and continue boiling for a further 2 minutes. Remove from the pan and refrigerate. When they have cooled, cut the lobsters in half lengthways with a strong knife. Remove the pyloric stomach, which is right at the front of the lobster near the eyes. Do the same with the crabs. Smash each of the claws as well, so they are easy for the diners to open. The langoustines are served as they are.

OTHER SHELLFISH AND GARNISH:
Finely chop the onion and mix with the red wine vinegar. This is for the oysters (not my favourite dressing, as I think it takes away too much of the oyster flavour). Cut the lemon and lime in wedges and remove the pips. Open the oysters and ease the muscle away from the shell. Open the scallops, clean the muscle, cut in thin strips and arrange on the flat scallop shells. Salt lightly with salt flakes. Arrange a lime wedge on each shell.

Arrange the shellfish on a large platter. Start with the prawns, then arrange the crab in a square in the middle. Arrange the lobster around the crab with the langoustines on top. Lay the scallops and oysters round the edge of the platter. Serve with freshly baked white bread, aïoli, mayonnaise, lemon , red wine vinegar and good quality butter.

Now for the steamed mussels …

WINE TIPS
In this dish, the determining flavour is the fresh taste of the sea from the shellfish. This goes well with a Muscadet from the Loire, a good quality Vinho Verde from northern Portugal or the classic Chablis. All of these have plenty of mineral and acid notes to go with the shellfish.

MUSSELS FOR THE SHELLFISH PLATTER

TO DRINK
Much of what was said about the seafood platter also applies here, but mussels on their own are also nice with beer. Weissbier is one of my favourites with mussels. Acid is important to break down the fat in the sauce.

½ kg/1 lb 2 oz mussels
1 garlic clove, finely chopped
1 shallot, finely chopped
1 sprig thyme, finely chopped
100 ml/3½ fl oz cream
a little oil for sautéing

Remove the byssal threads from the mussels and wash thoroughly in cold water. Discard any shells that are damaged or still open. Sauté the garlic, shallot and thyme in a little oil until the onion is transparent. Add the mussels and turn up the heat to maximum. Pour over the cream and mix well. Cover and cook for 3 minutes. Tip onto the shells and serve with the sauce from the pan.

AÏOLI & MAYONNAISE

AÏOLI:
1 egg
400 ml/14 fl oz neutral oil
1 clove garlic, finely chopped
1 tbsp Dijon mustard
2 tbsp red wine vinegar or sherry vinegar
salt and pepper

LEMON MAYONNAISE:
1 egg
400 ml/14 fl oz neutral oil
1 tbsp Dijon mustard
juice and grated zest of 1 lemon
salt and pepper

Make the mayonnaise and aïoli (using the same method for both). I often make mayonnaise in a food processor when making large quantities, but it's easy to make it with a whisk for a small quantity like this.

Whisk the egg, mustard and vinegar/lemon juice together thoroughly. Trickle in the oil, whisking all the time. It is important to add it a drop at a time to start with, to minimise the risk of splitting. When all the oil has been whisked in, the basis is ready.

For the aïoli, mix in finely chopped garlic. For the lemon mayonnaise, add the grated lemon zest. Season with salt and pepper and, if desired, add more lemon juice.

HOW TO MAKE MAYONNAISE:

1. Put eggs and mustard in a bowl.

2. Whisk by hand for about 2 minutes, until airy.

3. Add lemon juice and salt.

4. Drizzle in the oil in a thin stream, whisking continually. Beat in all the oil.

Left: Geir is down at the harbour on Fitjar to check fisherman Asbjørn Kleppe's catch.
Above: Shellfish party with good childhood friends on the patio at the family's boathouse on Fitjar. From the left: Line Kaksrud, Rune Gerhardsen, Geir, Kristine Sævdal og Leif Anders "Daffe" Aarbø.

GRILLED HALIBUT STEAKS, SUMMER SALAD AND NEW POTATOES WITH HORSERADISH SAUCE

SUMMER SALAD:
2 little gem lettuces
or 1 iceberg lettuce
1 cucumber
300 ml/10½ fl oz light sour cream
2 tbsp apple or white wine vinegar
1 tsp salt
1 tsp sugar
pepper

NEW POTATOES:
800 g/1 lb 12 oz
new potatoes
salt
a little dill, if desired

HORSERADISH SAUCE:
100 ml/3½ fl oz cream
200 g/7 oz butter
juice and grated
zest of ½ lemon
salt and pepper
1 tsp horseradish, grated
1 tbsp parsley, chopped

HALIBUT:
4 halibut steaks,
each about 300 g/10½ oz
1 lemon
salt and pepper
2 tbsp good quality olive oil

SUMMER SALAD:

Mix the sour cream with the vinegar, sugar, salt and a little pepper. Tear the lettuce in pieces or cut in rough strips. Peel the cucumber and cut in thin slices. I like to cut it with a potato peeler after removing the skin, because it gives you nice long slices. Mix the lettuce and cucumber into the sour cream dressing just before serving.

NEW POTATOES:

Cut the new potatoes in slices and boil in salted water with a little dill until tender. Cover with kitchen paper and set aside in a warm place.

HORSERADISH SAUCE:

This is a modified version of "sandefjordssmør" (sandefjord butter), to which I have added horseradish. Reduce the cream by half. Cut the butter in cubes and whisk into the cream. As you do this, you must take the pan off the heat occasionally, as this sauce mustn't boil or it will split. If the sauce splits, you can add a little cold water and whisk briskly, perhaps with a hand mixer. Season the sauce with lemon juice, grated lemon zest, grated horseradish, salt and pepper. Pour over the potatoes before serving and sprinkle with chopped parsley.

HALIBUT:

Salt and pepper the halibut steaks and pour over the oil. Place the fish on a hot grill rack and grill for 3–4 minutes on each side. Squeeze over a little lemon juice and top with a slice of lemon. If you grill lemon slices a little, it will bring out the taste of the juice.

HOW TO MAKE "SANDEFJORD BUTTER":

1. Reduce the cream by half.

2. Beat in the butter a little at a time.

3. Add grated horseradish, lemon juice and parsley. Horseradish doesn't really belong in Sandefjord butter, but I think it's nice!

WINE TIPS

This is a dish that needs a wine with plenty of body. Halibut is a fish with a lot of flavour, along with the butter in the sauce, the acid from the cucumber and sour cream salad, and a little sweetness from the new potatoes. A good, slightly oaky, Chardonnay from France, the western part of Australia, or South Africa will tackle this combination very well with good acidity and sweetness.

WHOLE ROAST DUCK TWO WAYS OF SERVING

2 ducks, each 2–3 kg/4½–9 lb
(farm reared, not wild. One duck would be sufficient for a
starter, but at Le Canard the rule was one duck for 2 people)

salt and pepper

Cut off the ends of the wings and the legs below the thigh. Truss the duck to hold the thighs in place and give the bird a nice compact shape. Rub with salt and pepper.

Roast on an oven tray at 230 °C/450 °F for 15 minutes. Reduce the heat to 180 °C/350 °F and roast for a further 30 minutes.

Set aside to rest in a warm place for 20 minutes before serving. This is important, as it allows the heat to spread evenly through the meat and all the juices are retained.

The duck may be returned to the oven for 2 minutes immediately before serving to add a little more heat.

Bring the duck to the table whole, perhaps garnished with a sprig of herbs, and carve at the table. Start by removing the thighs and then the breast. It takes a bit of practice to get it looking nice. While you are carving, you should have someone in the kitchen to prepare the garnish on the plates and bring them in when you have finished carving the meat …

HOW TO TRUSS A DUCK:

1. Truss the duck with string. The wings should be close to the body.

2. The thighs should be tied together tightly.

POUR THE PAN JUICES OVER THE DUCK:

While the duck is roasting in the oven it's a good idea to baste by spooning the pan juices over it 2–3 times. There's a lot of flavour in the fat, so you will make the duck tastier and juicier by spooning the fat over it during roasting.

97

DUCK WITH GLAZED TURNIPS AND ONIONS, SARLADAISE POTATOES AND ORANGE SAUCE

ORANGE SAUCE:
500 ml/18 fl oz reduced beef
stock/duck stock
2 oranges
½ lemon
1 tbsp sugar
1 small sprig thyme
2 tbsp butter
salt and pepper

SARLADAISE POTATOES:
500 g/1 lb 2 oz almond potatoes
1 tbsp parsley, finely chopped
4 tbsp fat from the roast duck
salt and pepper
1 tsp Dijon mustard

GLAZED VEGETABLES:
4 turnips
8 small onions
100 g/3½ oz asparagus beans
juice of 1 lemon
grated zest of ½ lemon
salt and pepper
1 tbsp butter
2 tbsp sugar

SAUCE:

Using a potato peeler, remove the thin orange layer of peel from the orange and reserve. Squeeze the juice from the orange and lemon. Make a caramel with the sugar (see page 48) and add the lemon and orange juice. Add the thyme and boil for 2 minutes. Add the reduced stock and simmer for 5 minutes. Add the orange peel and remove the pan from the heat. Strain after 10 minutes. It is important not to let it stand any longer, otherwise the peel will make the sauce taste bitter. To serve, warm up the sauce, stir in the butter, season with salt and pepper and if necessary adjust the acidity by adding a little more lemon juice.

POTATOES:

Bake the potatoes whole and in their skins at 180 °C/350 °F for 40 minutes until completely soft. Allow to cool a little before peeling. Mash with a fork in a saucepan and add the duck fat and mustard. Season with salt and pepper and add the parsley immediately before serving.

VEGETABLES:

Peel the onions and turnips, and cut the turnips in wedges. Cut away the dry ends of the asparagus beans. Bring a saucepan of lightly salted water to the boil. Cook the turnips for 1 minute, then plunge in iced water. Cook the asparagus beans for 3 minutes and plunge in iced water. Simmer the onions for 5 minutes. If they are overcooked, they will fall apart. Put the lemon peel, lemon juice and 2 tablespoons water in a saucepan with the sugar and butter. Bring to the boil and pour over the onions. Boil for 5 minutes, stirring a little to glaze the onions all over. Add the turnips and glaze together with the onions for a further 2 minutes. Season with salt and pepper and serve. Heat up the asparagus beans in a separate pan with a little butter, salt and pepper. Garnish the plates with vegetables and potatoes. Arrange the meat on top, and finally the sauce.

Blanching vegetables

When you blanch vegetables, it is important to have the water at a rolling boil and to plunge the vegetables in iced water as quickly as possible. You can use cold running water from the tap, if you don't have any ice. When the vegetables are cold, they should be removed from the water so they don't go soft and lose their flavour.

GLAZED DUCK THIGHS WITH LENTIL SALAD

DUCK THIGHS:
4 thighs cut from whole roast ducks
200 ml/7 fl oz orange sauce
(see page 98)

LENTIL SALAD:
160 g/5¾ oz green Puy lentils
400 ml/14 fl oz chicken stock
1 shallot, finely chopped
1 clove garlic, finely chopped
1 sprig thyme, finely chopped
1 tbsp good quality olive oil

4 spring onions, finely chopped

VINAIGRETTE:
1 tsp mustard
50 ml good quality olive oil
1 tsp red wine vinegar

DUCK THIGHS:
Remove the innermost bone from the duck thighs, so there is only one bone remaining in each thigh. Put the thighs in a saucepan with the sauce and simmer over low heat for 5 minutes while adding the sauce. The thighs will be nicely glazed and ready to serve.

Arrange the thighs in the middle of the plate, surrounded by lentil salad.

LENTILS:
Rinse the lentils in cold water in a sieve. Sauté the shallot, thyme and garlic in 1 tablespoon olive oil until the onion is transparent. Add the lentils and chicken stock. Simmer for about 10 minutes until the lentils are soft. Set aside to cool.

VINAIGRETTE:
Make the vinaigrette by whisking mustard and red wine vinegar and gradually adding olive oil to make a smooth dressing. Mix the spring onions with the lentils and the vinaigrette and season with salt and pepper.

WINE TIPS
These are rich dishes with quite a lot of fat from the duck and a little sweetness from the vegetables and sauce. Fruity French wines from Lirac or Gigondas in the southern Rhône or a wine from Priorat in Spain have plenty of fruity sweetness to counterbalance the vegetables and sauce and quite a lot of alcohol to combat the fat in the potatoes and meat.

WINE TIPS

Lamb is a very tasty meat, especially in dishes like this where the lamb fat is also used. The garnishes are typical of the Mediterranean area – Provence and Italy. A red wine from southern Italy, such as one made from Aglianico grapes, is very suitable. You can also choose a full-bodied wine from southern France based on Mourvèdre, Syrah and Grenache, perhaps from the areas of Corbières or Minervois.

For this dish you can prepare the sauce, cream and tomatoes the day before your guests arrive and do the rest immediately before serving.

RACK OF LAMB WITH BAKED TOMATOES AND AUBERGINE CAVIAR

RACK OF LAMB:
2 racks of lamb
(250–300 g/9–10½ oz per person)
2 cloves garlic
1 sprig rosemary
2 tbsp butter

BAKED TOMATOES:
8 nice small tomatoes
1 small sprig thyme, finely chopped
½ clove garlic, finely chopped
2 tbsp good quality olive oil
1 tsp sugar
½ tsp salt
pepper

AUBERGINE CREAM:
2 aubergines
1 clove garlic, finely chopped
½ tsp thyme, finely chopped
2 tbsp good quality olive oil
salt and pepper

POTATO GRATIN:
800 g/1 lb 12 oz almond potatoes
2 cloves garlic, finely chopped
2 shallots
300 ml/10 fl oz cream
1 sprig thyme
salt and pepper

LAMB SAUCE "DIABLE":
200 ml/7 fl oz reduced lamb stock
200 ml/7 fl oz reduced beef stock
1–2 pinches cayenne pepper
2 sprigs tarragon
2 shallots
4 tbsp good quality olive oil
50 ml/2 fl oz white wine
2 plum tomatoes

MUSHROOMS AND SPINACH:
250 g/9 oz spinach
1 clove garlic, finely chopped
1 shallot, finely chopped
1 tbsp butter
200 g/7 oz mushrooms
(wild, button or oyster mushrooms)

POTATO GRATIN:
Peel the potatoes and cut in thin slices. Cut the shallot and garlic in slices and sauté in a pan with the thyme. Add the cream and season with salt and pepper. Arrange the potato slices in layers in an ovenproof dish and pour over the cream. Bake in the oven at 180 °C/350 °F for 1 hour. The potatoes should be cooked through and golden on top.

BAKED TOMATOES:
Make a slit in the tops of the tomatoes, plunge in boiling water until the skins start to loosen and cool in iced water. Remove the skins and cut the tomatoes in two. Add the garlic, thyme, salt, pepper and sugar along with the olive oil. Dry in the oven on baking parchment at 100 °C/210 °F for 30 minutes.

AUBERGINE CREAM:
Bake the aubergines in the oven at 180 °C/350 °F for 40 minutes. They should be completely soft. Scrape out the flesh. Fry the chopped garlic and thyme in the olive oil. Add the aubergine flesh and cook for 10 minutes, to evaporate a little of the liquid. Whiz in a blender until smooth and season with salt and pepper.

LAMB SAUCE "DIABLE":
Cut away the base of the stalks from the plum tomatoes and cut a cross in the tops of the tomatoes. Plunge the tomatoes in boiling water until the skin starts to come away by the cuts, then in iced water to cool. Remove the skins. Cut each one in 4 wedges and remove the insides. Dice the remaining flesh and reserve for the sauce. Sauté the onion in olive oil with 1 sprig tarragon and cayenne pepper for the sauce. When the onion is transparent, pour over the white wine and reduce completely. Add the lamb and beef stock and boil for 10 minutes. Strain and season with salt and cayenne pepper. The flavour should be quite hot. Finely chop the remaining tarragon and add this and the diced tomato immediately before serving.

MUSHROOMS AND SPINACH:
Sauté the garlic and shallot in butter until transparent. Add the mushrooms and fry until golden. Add the spinach, heat, and season with salt and pepper. It is important not to heat the spinach for too long, otherwise it will turn to mush and lose its flavour.

RACK OF LAMB:
Brown the racks of lamb fat side down in the pan with the garlic and thyme. When they are golden on the fat side, turn and remove from the heat. Add a little butter, salt and pepper. Roast in the oven at 180 °C/350 °F for about. 8 minutes. Check that the meat is firm when you take them out. 55 °C/130 °F is a good internal temperature for the meat when you take it out of the oven. Let it rest for 10 minutes before serving.

FONDANT WITH GINGER PEARS AND SPICED ICE CREAM

FONDANT:
2 eggs
2 egg yolks
75 g/2¾ oz sugar
125 g/4 ½ oz butter
125 g/4 ½ oz dark chocolate
50 g/1 ¾ oz flour

GINGER PEARS:
2 pears
100 g/3½ oz sugar
1 cm/½ inch fresh ginger
juice of ½ lemon
100 ml/3½ fluid oz water

SPICED ICE CREAM:
5 egg yolks
300 ml/10 fl oz whole milk
200 ml/7 fl oz cream
130 g/4½ oz sugar
2 star anis
1 cinnamon stick (preferably Ceylon, as it has the most flavour)
3 whole green cardamoms
¼ vanilla pod
60 g/2 oz glucose

FONDANT:
Melt the butter and chocolate in the microwave over low heat or in a bain-marie. Whisk together the eggs, egg yolks and sugar. They don't need to be very airy, just thoroughly mixed. Add to the melted chocolate mixture. Sift over the flour and mix in. Grease ring moulds or muffin tins (line with baking parchment to make sure the fondant doesn't stick), and fill them with the mixture. These can be kept in the refrigerator for up to 2 weeks or frozen. Bake at 180 °C/350 °F for 15 minutes. The fondant should be liquid inside.

GINGER PEARS:
Bring the sugar and water to the boil. Peel the ginger and cut in thin slices. Add the ginger and lemon juice to the syrup.

Peel the pears, cut into 8 wedges and remove the seeds. Put the pears in the syrup and weigh them down with something to keep them under the syrup. Simmer over low heat for 15–20 minutes. They should be soft all through. Leave to cool in the syrup. Cut in pieces before serving. You could reduce a little of the syrup to serve with the pears.

SPICED ICE CREAM:
Bring the milk, glucose and cream to the boil with all the spices. Mix briefly with a hand mixer to bring out the flavour of the spices. Set aside to draw for 1 hour. Beat together the egg yolks and sugar and add the spiced milk. Heat to 85 °C/180 °F. If you dip a wooden spoon in the "custard" and run a finger through it, it should leave a dry strip. Strain the custard, cool, stir and freeze in an ice cream maker.

Choose your own mould

Chocolate fondant can be baked in any kind of mould that can withstand heat – for example in disposable foil containers.

WINE TIPS

Chocolate and wine are a bit of a difficult combination, as it's hard to match the strong flavours and sweetness of the chocolate. In this recipe it is also combined with a little fruit and spicy ice cream. The red dessert wine Mas Amiel from south-west France can cope with this problem. It has enough sweetness and a few of the same spicy notes as the ice cream and the acid that is in the fruit. A Tokaji with a sweetness of at least 5 puttunyos can also work well.

PAVLOVA WITH STRAWBERRIES AND VANILLA CREAM

PAVLOVA (MERINGUE):
150 g/5½ oz egg whites
140 g/5 oz sugar
140 g/5 oz icing sugar

VANILLA CREAM:
100 g/3½ oz white chocolate
2 leaves gelatine
500 ml/18 fl oz cream
½ vanilla pod

STRAWBERRY GRANITA:
200 g/7 oz strawberries
2 tbsp sugar
2 tbsp water

ELDERFLOWER JELLY:
5 elderflower heads
200 ml/7 fl oz water
40 g/1½ oz sugar
2 leaves gelatine

For Serving:
200 g/7 oz strawberries

PAVLOVA (MERINGUE):
Beat the egg whites at low speed for 15 minutes. After beating for 5 minutes, gradually add the sugar. When you have finished beating, fold in the sifted icing sugar. Pipe the mixture onto baking parchment in thick strips of the desired length. Bake at 100 °C/210 °F for 40 minutes. Cool. Will keep for a long time in the freezer in an airtight container.

VANILLA CREAM:
Soak the gelatine. Heat the cream, softened gelatine and vanilla pod and simmer for 30 minutes. Break the white chocolate in pieces and melt in the cream. Cool and beat together. Chill before serving.

GRANITA:
Whiz all the ingredients in a blender and freeze in a container. Mash with a fork or spoon before serving.

ELDERFLOWER JELLY:
Soak the gelatine. Bring the water, sugar and softened gelatine to the boil, add the elderflowers and simmer for 10 minutes. Strain, transfer to a container and refrigerate. To serve, cut in cubes.

SERVING:
Stand the pavlova bars on a little vanilla cream to keep them upright. Chill the vanilla cream. Cut up the strawberries, arrange on the plates and top with jelly and granita.

ELDERFLOWER LEMONADE:
1 litre/1¾ pints water
200 g/7 oz sugar
10 elderflower heads
1 lemon
4 strawberries

Bring the water and sugar to the boil, remove from the heat and add the elderflowers. Leave to draw for 10 minutes, strain and flavour with lemon juice. Cool and serve with ice cubes and perhaps a few pieces of strawberry.

WINE TIPS
A nice, fresh dessert with a slight sweetness from the meringue. Moscato d'Asti from Piedmont in northern Italy is perfect with this dish. It is nice and sweet, yet still fresh because is has acid notes and is slightly sparkling. This is the ultimate wine for strawberries in summer. Other possible choices are sweet champagne or and Eiswein from Austria or Germany, made from Riesling or Huxelrebe grapes.

THE MAN WHO CONJURES WITH FLAVOURS

Sour, sweet, salty, bitter – these are the four main flavours that must come together and harmonise. Bass with treble, minor with major, but how could Geir find out whether a flavour would hit the right note? He had worked at a Michelin-starred restaurant in Paris and learned how to select the basic ingredients. He had worked at Le Canard in Oslo and learned how to turn a carrot into a miniature work of art. But he needed to understand more about how flavours work on the tongue.

He knew who would be able to teach him – Odd Ivar Solvold, the star chef in Sandefjord, who had won bronze in the Bocuse d'Or. Whatever Geir wants, he gets, and not many weeks went by before he was offered a job as chef with Solvold. He took his sailing boat with him and moved to the quayside in Sandefjord.

"Why do you do it like that?" No-one had ever responded so positively to all his questions. And no-one had ever given so many right answers. Geir could ask about the strangest things that were more to do with chemistry than food, and Odd Ivar Solvold would know the answer. He knew that if you boil carrots with orange juice in the water, the carrots will never finish cooking. He knew that if you boil a red onion and it loses its colour, you can get the colour back by adding lemon.

Odd Ivar tasted and explained. Geir tasted the same things and understood. He learned how to distinguish the different flavours in a dish. How to recognise minute nuances. Is it too bitter? Do I need to add a quarter of a teaspoon of sugar? Should I add a little less water to the stock next time?

He concentrated hard on his work, but not so hard that he didn't notice the pretty young girl who stood next to him making desserts. He thought she was very chatty, but that was all right, because he didn't talk very much himself.

Katrine – that was her name – was just as determined as Geir once she had made up her mind about something. She didn't give way at all until the stoical young man from western Norway finally asked:

"Would you like to come home with me and see my sailing boat?"

AGED 22–28

Two star chefs in Solvold's kitchen in Sandefjord. – "No-one has taught me more about flavours than Odd Ivar", says Geir.

3 KINDS ᵒꜰ FINGER FOOD

BRANDADE

BAKED SALMON

FRESH BRANDADE ON CROUTONS
WITH OLIVES:
1 cod belly or tail
1 clove garlic
1 sprig thyme
zest of 1 lemon
3 tbsp good quality olive oil
salt and black pepper

Bake the fish in the oven with oil, lemon zest, thyme and garlic at 120 °C/250 °F until cooked through. Remove from the oven and whiz in a blender or whisk with the oil until smooth and creamy. Season with salt and pepper. Spoon the brandade onto croutons made by baking thin slices of baguette in the oven with olive oil, and top with pieces of olive.

BAKED SALMON WITH
CAULIFLOWER AND CAPERS:
200 g/7 oz salmon fillets
1 tsp sugar
1 tsp salt
1 small baguette
good quality olive oil

½ cauliflower
50 ml/2 fl oz cream
1 tsp grated lemon zest
salt
1 tbsp capers
1 hard boiled egg
1 tsp tarragon

Sprinkle the salmon fillets with salt and sugar and refrigerate for at least 2 hours. Bake at 40 °C/100 °F for 40 minutes. May be served hot or cold.

Cut the baguette in thin slices and drizzle with good quality olive oil. Bake in the oven at 180 °C/350 °F for 8–10 minutes until crisp and golden.

Boil the cauliflower until tender. Drain and whiz in a blender with the cream and grated lemon zest. Season with salt. Mix in the capers, tarragon and chopped hard boiled egg by hand. Spread the mixture on the crispy bread and top with a slice of salmon.

PRAWNBURGERS

PRAWNBURGERS WITH CURRY AND CELERIAC:
500 g/1 lb 2 oz uncooked prawns
1 tsp tarragon, chopped
grated lemon zest
oil for frying

300 g/10½ oz celeriac
1 tbsp butter
curry to taste
ginger to taste

WINE TIPS

This is food to accompany apéritifs, probably eaten standing when the guests arrive. Champagne or a good Franciacorta from Lombardy in northern Italy are just the thing. They have the acidity to cleanse the palate and are just right for that stage of the meal.

Boil 200 g/7 oz celeriac in lightly salted water until tender. Whiz in a blender with the butter until smooth. Season with salt, pepper and grated lemon zest.

Dice the remaining celeriac and boil in lightly salted water until tender. Turn in a little good quality olive oil, lemon and salt before serving.

Peel and roughly chop the prawns. Mix with the tarragon and lemon zest. Press the mixture into rounds and fry in a hot pan with cooking oil. Season with salt and pepper and add a little butter just before you finish frying. Top the burgers with creamed and diced celeriac before serving. May be served with a light curry foam based on the prawn soup (see page 81), with the addition of a little fried curry powder and ginger.

"I have travelled a lot in Thailand, and I love eating Thai fast food with fresh ingredients and lots of chilli, lime and coriander."

SOM TAM

1 large unripe papaya
1 unripe mango
50 g/1¾ oz peanuts (preferably unsalted)
8 nice small tomatoes
½ red chilli pepper
2 cloves garlic
¼ onion, thinly sliced
1 sprig coriander
3 tbsp fish sauce
1 lime

Toast the peanuts in a dry pan until golden. Peel the papaya and mango and cut in thin strips. Cut the tomatoes in two and put them in a bowl or a mortar with the garlic, chilli, lime juice, onion and fish sauce. Crush well together. Mix in the papaya, mango and coriander. Flavour with fish sauce, lime and chilli to suit your own taste. Sprinkle with roughly chopped peanuts before serving.

This makes a very good salad to go with chicken or seafood. Perfect with barbecued food. If you want to make it more European in style, you can also mix in a little iceberg or little gem lettuce.

TO DRINK
Beer is the only possibility here, preferably a slightly bitter Thai pilsner such as Chang or Tiger Beer from Singapore.

TOM YAM GUNG

BOUILLON:
800 ml/1½ pints chicken stock
4 tbsp fish sauce
1 lime
3 cm/1¼ ins ginger or galangal
½ red chilli pepper
1 stalk lemon grass
4 lime leaves
6 nice small tomatoes
8 small onions
1 clove garlic

GARNISH:
200 g/7 oz mushrooms, cut in big triangles
1 carrot, thinly sliced
2 spring onions, thinly sliced
16 scampi, peeled
1 large sprig coriander

Bring all the ingredients for the bouillon to the boil and simmer over low heat for 10 minutes.

Add the vegetables and scampi and simmer for a further 3–4 minutes. Add more lime juice, chilli and fish sauce to taste. It's just a question of finding the taste you like best.

Fish sauce on its own doesn't smell very nice, but it tastes delicious in Thai food. Fish sauce is the Thais' salt.

TO DRINK
Beer works best as a thirst-quencher with this. Choose a type of pilsner or a slightly bitter Pale Ale.

TUNA NIÇOISE

TUNA:
200 g/7 oz raw tuna
½ lemon
salt flakes and pepper
1 tbsp good quality olive oil

POACHED EGGS:
8 quails' eggs
2 tbsp white wine vinegar

CROUTONS:
4 wafer thin slices bread
1 tbsp good quality olive oil

BAKED TOMATOES:
8 nice small tomatoes
2 tbsp good quality olive oil
1 tsp sugar
½ tsp salt
pepper
1 small sprig thyme,
finely chopped
½ garlic clove,
finely chopped

GARNISH:
1 piquillo pepper
1 tbsp capers
8 anchovies
in olive oil
8 leaves basil
8 nice olives

WINE TIPS
This dish is typical of Provence. Really good rosé wines go very well with the tuna, tomatoes and olives. Try a rosé from the Tavel area or a pure blanc de blancs champagne, which has the acidity to complement the tomatoes and the salt in the olives and anchovies.

TUNA:
Cut the tuna in thin slices and arrange on the plate. Dress with lemon juice, olive oil, salt and pepper immediately before serving.

POACHED EGGS:
Break the quails' eggs carefully into a bowl. It's a good idea to use a small knife to make a hole in the shell, but take care not to stick it into the yolk. Add the white wine vinegar and a little water to the bowl with the eggs and leave for 10 minutes. This makes the egg white set little so that the eggs stay nice and round when you poach them. Drain the eggs carefully in a fine-meshed sieve. Bring water to the boil and tip in the eggs when it is just below boiling point. Simmer the eggs for 1.5 minutes – the yolks should be fluid. Cool in iced water. They can be kept for up to a week in lightly salted water in a refrigerator.

BAKED TOMATOES:
Cut a slit in the tops of the tomatoes and boil until the skins start to come away a little. Cool in iced water. Peel away the skins and cut the tomatoes in two. Add the garlic, thyme, salt, pepper and sugar along with the olive oil. Bake gently in the oven on baking parchment at 100 °C/210 °F for 1 hour.

CROUTONS:
Make the croutons by laying the slices of bread on baking parchment and drizzling with the olive oil. Bake at 170 °C/325 °F for 8–10 minutes until crisp and golden. Divide into smaller pieces before serving.

Cut the piquillo pepper in strips.

Arrange everything as a salad on top of the tuna.

KING CRAB WITH CAULIFLOWER AND SOYA

KING CRAB:
2 large Kamchatka king crabs
1 sprig tarragon, chopped
grated zest of ½ lemon
2 tbsp butter

3 KINDS OF CAULIFLOWER:
1 cauliflower
2 tbsp sour cream
salt and pepper
½ lemon
1 tbsp good quality olive oil

SOYA BUTTER:
4 tbsp butter
2 tbsp soy sauce
1 shallot

KING CRAB:
Remove the Kamchatka crabs from their shells. Make sure you also remove the bone that goes through the middle of the flesh. Wrap rolls of crab meat in plastic film and knot the ends. Put these in water at 80–90 °C/175–195 °F for 5 minutes. This gives the crab meat a nicer shape and makes it easier to fry. Remove the plastic film before frying the crab. Just before serving, put the butter in a hot pan before adding the crab. Fry until lightly golden all round. Add the grated lemon zest and tarragon at the last moment. Divide the crab into 8 pieces and serve.

3 KINDS OF CAULIFLOWER:
Cut the cauliflower down the middle and cut a few thin slices to give 4 thin "trees" of cauliflower. Cut the green parts of the cauliflower in slices using a mandolin or a cheese slice, to give you long, thin leaves. Boil the remainder of the cauliflower in water until just tender. Strain off the water (reserving a little for the foam) and whiz in a blender with the sour cream. Flavour with salt, pepper, grated lemon zest and lemon juice. Take a little of this "cream" and mix with a little of the cauliflower water and milk. Heat and beat to a foam with a hand mixer just before serving. Fry the cauliflower trees in a little oil until golden and dress them with lemon juice, lemon zest and salt.

SOYA BUTTER:
Finely chop the shallot and fry in butter until the butter is brown. Add the soy sauce.

FLAT TREES OF CAULIFLOWER
First make a completely straight cut lengthwise through the cauliflower stems. Use a mandolin to make small, flat trees out of the cauliflower.

WINE TIPS
Fried kind crab and cauliflower together have mild flavours. In this recipe, the soya supplies the salt, which counterbalances the sweetness of the crab. The perfect wine to go with this is a dry Riesling with plenty of fruitiness and high acidity. The wine takes a little of the sweetness from the crab, and the acidity is refreshing. Rheingau, Pfalz or Nahe in Germany are good regions for this type of pure Riesling.

paella + risotto = paellotto

MONKFISH WITH BASIL AND PAELLOTTO

MONKFISH:
2 sprigs basil
500 g/1 lb 2 oz monkfish fillets
½ dl good quality olive oil
grated zest of ½ lemon

GAZPACHO:
2 canned plum tomatoes
½ cucumber, peeled
juice of ½ lemon
1 small shallot
½ clove garlic
1 baked paprika
a little chilli
½ lemon
salt and pepper
sugar

PAELLOTTO:
100 g/3½ oz risotto rice
½ yellow onion
2 tbsp good quality olive oil
1 pinch saffron
approx. 500 ml/18 fl oz fish stock, mussel stock or chicken stock
50 g/1¾ oz parmesan
200 g/7 oz mussels
salt and black pepper
lemon

MONKFISH:
Whiz the basil, oil and lemon zest in a blender to a smooth oil. Rub the monkfish with this oil and let it marinate for at least 30 minutes. Bake in the oven at 150 °C/300 °F for 8–10 minutes. Check that it is firm, and then it's ready. The internal temperature should be 54-55 °C/130 °F. Season with salt and pepper. May be served hot or cold.

GAZPACHO:
Grind all the ingredients finely in a blender and flavour with salt, pepper, lemon and sugar. Squeeze the mixture through a cloth or a tea towel and heat before serving.

PAELLOTTO:
Clean and rinse the mussels. Put them in an empty saucepan, cover and steam over high heat for 3 minutes until all the shells have opened. Strain the stock into the fish stock. Remove the flesh from the shells and refrigerate. Fry the onion in olive oil with the saffron until transparent. Add the rice and heat until it begins to sizzle. Add enough hot stock to just cover the rice. Reduce then dilute with more stock. Stir gently so the rice doesn't stick. Boil for about 18 minutes, then the rice should be ready. Remove from the heat and season with parmesan, salt, pepper and lemon. Add the mussels and serve.

HOW TO MAKE RISOTTO:

1. Put plenty of olive oil in the pan and bring to medium heat. Then add finely chopped onion and saffron. Fry the onion in the oil until tender.

2. Tip in the risotto rice and stir into the oil. All the rice grains should be coated with oil. Fry the rice gently in the oil until it begins to sizzle.

3. Heat the stock in a saucepan before using. Pour the hot stock into the rice, stirring at regular intervals. Add the stock a little at a time, not all at once.

4. The risotto should boil for 18–20 minutes. Stir occasionally. Check the rice to see if it is ready. It should be soft, but slightly resistant.

COD FLAKES IN PUMPKIN SOUP

COD:
600 g/1 lb 4 oz cod loin
2 cloves garlic
4 tbsp good quality olive oil
salt and black pepper

CROUTONS:
4 wafer thin slices bread
1 tbsp good quality olive oil

SOUP:
800 g/1 lb 12 oz pumpkin
200 ml/7 fl oz crème fraîche
1 litre/1¾ pints fish stock
salt and black pepper

COD:
Salt and pepper the cod. Finely chop the garlic and sprinkle
over the fish along with good quality olive oil. Bake in the oven at
100 °C/210 °F until the fish flakes when presed. Split into flakes and
serve.

CROUTONS:
Make the croutons by laying the slices of bread on baking parchment
and drizzling with the olive oil. Bake at 170 °C/325 °F for 8–10
minutes until crisp and golden. Divide into smaller pieces before
serving.

SOUP:
Boil the pumpkin in the fish stock until tender. Whiz in a blender
with the crème fraîche. Season with salt, pepper and perhaps a little
lemon juice. Serve!

WINE TIPS
Cod is a lean, mild-flavoured fish, and here it's
combined with pumpkin, which has a slightly
nutty flavour and quite a lot of fat and
sweetness. Chardonnay-based wines with a
little oakiness go well with it, as they have a
slightly nutty, buttery taste. Burgundy is a good
tip, but try wines from New Zealand or North
America too, for instance from Oregon or
Washington State.

You could add a few toasted pumpkin seeds to the soup.

Plum tomatoes have firmer flesh and are easier to peel and dice. Ordinary tomatoes are softer than plum tomatoes and more likely to fall apart.

WINE TIPS

Asparagus has a slightly "green" taste, while the ham is salty and the tomatoes add tartness. The goat cheese also adds a little fat. Sauvignon blanc-based wines from the Loire (Pouilly-Fumé) or New Zealand have a bit of the same "green" taste and the acidity to counterbalance the fat and the tomatoes.

"When the first Norwegian asparagus arrives in the kitchen, I use it in everything!"

NORWEGIAN ASPARAGUS WITH HAM AND GOAT CHEESE CREAM

BREAD AND HAM:
4 thin slices white bread
100 g/3½ oz thin slices good ham (parma, serrano, San Daniele)

ASPARAGUS:
12 green asparagus
½ lemon
salt flakes
pepper
sugar
basil (preferably various kinds, such as lemon , red and common)

ASPARAGUS OIL:
50 ml/2 fl oz neutral oil
peel from the asparagus

FRESH GOAT CHEESE CREAM:
100 g/3½ oz fresh goat cheese
1 tsp basil

TOMATO SALSA:
2 ripe plum tomatoes
2 tbsp good quality olive oil

BREAD AND HAM:
Cut 4 thin slices of bread (1–2 mm/1/8 inch thick) with a food slicer or a sharp knife. It is easiest to do this when the bread is half frozen. Slice the ham as thinly as possible too.

ASPARAGUS:
Peel the bottom of the asparagus and boil for 2–3 minutes. It should be al dente. Plunge the asparagus straight into iced water to cool.

Before serving, flavour the asparagus with grated lemon zest, lemon juice, asparagus oil, salt and pepper.

ASPARAGUS OIL:
Whiz the peel from the asparagus with 50 ml/2 fl oz neutral oil in a blender until completely green. Then boil up, strain and cool.

FRESH GOAT CHEESE CREAM:
Beat the fresh goat cheese with 1 teaspoon finely chopped basil until creamy.

TOMATO SALSA:
Cut the base of the stalk out of the plum tomatoes and cut a cross in the tops. Put the tomatoes in boiling water until the skin begins to come away at the cuts. Plunge the tomatoes in iced water to cool. Remove the skins. Divide each into 4 wedges and scoop out the seeds. Dice the flesh and season with salt, pepper, olive oil and a little sugar.

HOW TO COOK ASPARAGUS:

1. Peel the lowest part of the asparagus that doesn't have fresh, green skin.

2. Cut off the lowest part with the white flesh – this may vary from nothing to 3–4 centimeter/1¼–1½ inches.

3. Bring the water to the boil and put in the asparagus. Use a large saucepan with plenty of water.

4. I like to blanch the asparagus in unsalted water, because if you salt the water you will lose some of the colour if you want to keep the asparagus.

CHICKEN IN MOREL BOUILLON

BOUILLON:
600 ml/1 pint chicken stock
100 g/3½ oz fresh morels (or 20 g/¼ oz dried morels)
100 g/3½ oz button mushrooms
1 tbsp neutral oil
salt and pepper
2 egg whites

SPRING VEGETABLES AND CHICKEN:
2 sticks celery
8 green asparagus
2 carrots
¼ celeriac
100 g/3½ oz peas
½ spring cabbage
1 tbsp good quality olive oil
100 g/3½ oz morels
4 skinless chicken breasts
1 sprig tarragon
salt and pepper

BOUILLON:
Sauté the mushrooms in the oil. Add the chicken stock, bring to the boil and simmer for 30 minutes. Strain and cool. Beat in the egg whites with a hand mixer, bring the stock back to the boil and continue boiling for 2 minutes. It will foam up a lot because of the egg whites. We do this to clarify the stock so it becomes transparent. Strain the stock through a fine sieve. Season the bouillon with salt and pepper.

SPRING VEGETABLES AND CHICKEN:
Peel the carrots, celeriac, celery and the bottom of the asparagus. Cut these vegetables and the cabbage in 3–4 cm/1¼–1½ inch pieces. All the vegetables are to be cooked in the bouillon. Start with the hardest, such as carrots and celeriac, together with the chicken breasts. Boil for 5 minutes before adding the remaining vegetables and the tarragon. Simmer for a further 3 minutes. Season again, as the vegetables take some of the salt out of the bouillon. Serve the chicken in deep plates with the bouillon.

WINE TIPS
Here we have light, mild flavours with almost no fat. Morels have a slightly earth and nutty aroma, while the vegetables have sweetness. The problem here is the bouillon, which quickly washes any drink away. Sherry is the classic accompaniment to bouillon. Amontillado or Palo Cortado work well. A full-bodied cava or blanc de noirs champagne with a slight oaky note can also be very good.

Asparagus skin for soup
Don't throw away the asparagus skin, as you can make nice soup from it. Put the skins in a saucepan and add enough milk just to cover them. Boil for one 1 minute. Then whiz the soup in a blender. Strain and flavour with salt, pepper and grated nutmeg. You could add pieces of fish or asparagus.

"Dinner tastes especially good when you've shot it yourself. Here I was shooting seabirds."

SPICE-FRIED EIDER DUCK WITH FRUIT AND SPICE COUSCOUS AND HAZELNUT BUTTER

2 eider ducks (preferably recently shot!) or other ducks
toasted coriander seeds, star anis, cinnamon and
ground black pepper
4 tbsp butter
50 g/1¾ oz hazelnuts
150 g/5½ oz couscous (medium)
100 g/3½ grapes
200 g/7 oz dried fruit (raisins, figs, apricots, prunes)
1 nice apple
500 ml/18 fl oz chicken stock
1 shallot
100 g/3½ oz leeks

Fry the shallot with 1 teaspoon of the mixed spices in 2 tablespoons butter. Add all the dried fruit, grapes, leeks and roughly chopped apple. Add the couscous, pour over the chicken stock, bring to the boil, cover and set aside for 5–10 minutes. Season with salt and flavour with the mixed spices and perhaps a little butter before serving.

Brown the duck breasts over high heat. Reduce the heat and add the butter, nuts, salt and mixed herbs. Spoon the butter over the meat and turn occasionally. Check during cooking. The meat should be quite firm before you remove it from the pan (after about 5 minutes). Let it rest for 5 minutes before cutting and serving.

VEAL ENTRECÔTE WITH ROASTED VEGETABLES

ROASTED VEGETABLES:
½ kohl rabi
2 carrots
1 parsnips
½ celeriac
2 tbsp olive oil
rosemary
salt and pepper
1 clove garlic

VEAL:
800 g/1 lb 12 oz veal entrecôte (you can also use beef)
1 tbsp rosemary, finely chopped
grated zest of ½ lemon
2 tbsp butter
salt and pepper

CEP FOAM:
50 g/1¾ oz ceps, dried
1 shallot, chopped
100 ml//3½ fl oz dry white wine
500 ml/18 fl oz chicken stock
300 ml/10 fl oz cream
salt and pepper

CABBAGE AND MUSHROOMS:
1 oxheart cabbage or spring cabbage
300 g/10½ oz button mushrooms or ceps
2 shallots, sliced
2 tbsp butter
salt and pepper

ASPARAGUS BEANS:
150 g//5½ oz asparagus beans
1 clove garlic
salt
1 tbsp butter

ROASTED VEGETABLES:

Cut the vegetables to the desired size and blanch al dente in lightly salted water. Put the vegetables on a baking sheet with rosemary, garlic and olive oil, and roast at 180 °C/350 °F until tender. It is important to turn the vegetables during roasting so they cook evenly.

VEAL:

Brown the meat whole. Heat a frying pan and add a little neutral oil when it begins to smoke. Fry the meat well on all sides. It is important to brown the meat well, as that is what gives it the nice meaty flavour. It's not to keep the juices in, it's for the sake of the flavour. Then add the rosemary, lemon zest and butter and remove from the heat. Place the meat in a ovenproof dish and pour over the butter with the herbs and lemon juice. Season with salt and pepper and roast in the oven at 180 °C/350 °F for 25 minutes. The internal temperature should be 53 °C/127 °F for veal and 50 °C/122 °F for beef. Remember that the temperature will rise by at least 5 degrees C/9 °F while the meat is resting. Let it rest for 20 minutes and warm in the oven for 2 minutes before cutting it in 4 large slices for serving.

CEP FOAM:

Sauté the onion until slightly foaming. Break up the ceps with your fingers and add to the pan. Pour over the white wine and reduce the liquid completely. Add the stock and reduce by half. Add the cream and boil for 5 minutes. Season with salt and pepper, and mix thoroughly with a hand mixer. Strain. Bring to the boil and foam with a hand mixer before serving. When foaming sauces, it is important to have the sauce at about 70–80 °C/160–175 °F rather than at boiling point so the foam will last longer.

CABBAGE AND MUSHROOMS:

Roughly chop the cabbage and blanch for 1 minute. Sauté the onion in butter with the mushrooms, add the cabbage and heat through. Season with salt and pepper.

ASPARAGUS BEANS:

Boils the asparagus beans in lightly salted water for 3 minutes and plunge in iced water. Sauté the beans with a little butter and finely chopped garlic before serving, to give a little extra flavour.

WINE TIPS

Veal is a mild-flavoured meat, but in this dish there is a little fat with it. The vegetables are roasted, which brings out a lot of sweetness, and the sauce is made with cream and ceps. For this dish we need tannic acid to counteract the meat juices and the fat, and fruit sweetness to balance the vegetables. Wines under 10 years old from the west side of the Bordeaux region are excellent, or we can go to Tuscany in Italy for a Chianti Riserva or a vino nobile from Montepulciano, also under 10 years old.

HOW TO FOAM SAUCES:
When you foam sauces, it is important that the sauce is not at boiling point, but heated to about 70–80 °C/160–175 ºF. Then the foam will last better. Use a hand-mixer, hold the saucepan at an angle and mix for one minute.

CHOCOLATE SANDWICH WITH PINEAPPLE SORBET

CHOCOLATE BASE:
60 g/2 oz sugar
25 ml/1 fl oz water
1 egg
45 g/1¾ oz butter, cubed,
at room temperature
70 g/2¾ oz dark chocolate
(min. 55% cocoa content)

CHOCOLATE MOUSSE:
2 egg yolks
50 ml/2 fl oz whipping cream
30g/1¼ oz sugar
100g/3½ oz dark chocolate
200 ml/7 fl oz whipping cream
(with perhaps a ristretto – a small
shot of espresso – to flavour)

PINEAPPLE SORBET:
½ nice pineapple
50 g/1¾ oz sugar
50 ml/2 fl oz water
½ tsp black pepper

CARAMELLISED PINEAPPLE:
½ nice pineapple
50 g/1¾ oz sugar
½ tsp black pepper
20 ml/1 1/3 tbsp brown rum

CHOCOLATE BASE:
Boil the sugar and water for 2 minutes. Put the chocolate, butter and egg in a small blender and pour in the hot sugar syrup. Mix together to a smooth mass. Pour the mixture into a mould about 20 cm x 5 cm/8 x 2 inches and bake at 150 °C/300 °F for 8 minutes. Refrigerate.

CHOCOLATE MOUSSE:
Bring 50 ml/2 fl oz whipping cream, egg yolks and sugar to the boil, whisking all the time. It should only just bubble. Add the chocolate and allow to melt in the mixture. Cool to body temperature. Whip 200 ml/7 fl oz cream and fold into the chocolate mixture. Pour onto the chocolate base and freeze. Cut into the desired shape and arrange on the plates. Allow to thaw for 10–15 minutes before serving.

PINEAPPLE SORBET:
Bring the sugar and water to the boil and then refrigerate. Peel the pineapple, cut rough cubes and freeze. Before serving, whiz the pineapple in a food processor with the black pepper. Dilute with sugar syrup to give a nice sorbet consistency.

CARAMELLISED PINEAPPLE:
Cut the pineapple in cubes. Heat a pan and add the pineapple, together with the sugar, rum and pepper. Let the sugar caramellise around the pineapple.

You can use all kinds of frozen berries and fruit in a sorbet.

HOW TO MAKE PINEAPPLE SORBET:

1. Cut the pineapple in chunks and freeze. Put the frozen chunks straight into a blender or food processor.

2. Add sugar syrup to the pineapple with the blender running and mix until you get a nice consistency.

WINE TIPS
This is a slightly lighter chocolate dessert with a lot of fruitiness and tartness from the sorbet and pineapple. An eiswein, trockenbeerenauslese or a very sweet beerenauslese from the Mosel or Rheingau regions of Germany or Neusiedlersee in Austria are excellent, with a little of the same tropical aromas, sweetness and tartness.

RIS À L'AMANDE

MAZARIN:
250 g/9 oz marzipan
250 g/9 oz butter
250 g/9 oz sugar
½ vanilla pod
60 g/2 oz cornflour
250 g/9 oz eggs

CHERRIES:
500 g1 lb 2 oz cherries
150 g/5½ oz sugar
50 ml/2 fl oz water
1 star anis
1 cinnamon stick
¼ vanilla pod
1 tsp potato flour

RICE:
300 ml/10 fl oz rice porridge
(pudding rice boiled in water and milk)
300 ml/10 fl oz cream
2 tbsp sugar
50 g/1¾ oz almonds, chopped and scalded
1 tbsp almond liqueur (Amaretto)

MAZARIN:
Mix all the dry ingredients with the butter in a food processor, then add the eggs one at a time. Transfer the mixture to a 30 x 40 cm/12 x 16 inch mould lined with baking parchment and bake at 150 °C/300 °F for about 30 minutes. This can also be baked in bread tins. The important thing is that the cake should be about 2–3 cm/¾–1¼ ins thick.

CHERRIES:
Put the sugar, water, star anis, vanilla and cinnamon in a saucepan and bring to the boil. Add the cherries and simmer over low heat for 10 minutes. Thicken with potato flour mixed with water. Leave the cherries to cool in the syrup.

RICE:
Whip the cream and sugar until airy. Fold in the rice and add the Amaretto and almonds. Serve in glasses with cherries at the bottom, then rice and cherries on top, and a bar of the mazarin cake.

WINE TIPS
This dish is associated with Christmas, so we need a little alcohol, which is also good to counterbalance the fat on the creamed rice. Malvasia Madeira are good for this, as they have a slight almond note too, or a Marsala from southern Italy.

EATING COMPETI-
TIONS AND
OTHER
CONTESTS

Geir has always enjoyed competing. For instance with his friend Rune, to see who could eat the most pistachio ice cream. They were 14 years old and had each bought a two-litre tub at the SPAR grocery shop on Fitjar. Geir ate the most, won and wasn't sick. Rune ate the least, lost and was sick. Geir still likes the pistachio flavour. Rune doesn't.

Stuffing yourself with ice cream is easier than winning cooking competitions, because the dishes in these competitions don't only have to taste perfect, they have to be made with surgical precision as well. For example, if your hands tremble a little when you are arranging the dessert, a wafer-thin caramel creation may crash land in the cream. Then you have a problem. You also lose points if one cube of basil jelly is bigger than another. So there are many things that can go wrong.

Geir had plenty of experience of the fact that a lot can go wrong. For instance, he twice took part in "Young Chef of the Year", and things went so badly, especially the first time, that Geir was grumpy for several days afterwards. But with Odd Ivar Solvold as his coach, he suddenly found himself with a gold medal round his neck in 2003. He had won the Norwegian Championship!

NORWEGIAN CHAMPION. The words tasted better than the finest ingredients, better than Fitjar cod and Sandefjord asparagus put together. Now he could take the Bocuse d'Or star down from the sky, look at it and polish it. Now it was no longer just an unattainable dream but a real objective.

In 2007 he became Chef of the year. In 2008 he outclassed all the other competitors and became European Champion. That was great. So great he could hardly believe it. Now there was only one final competition left to win: the Bocuse d'Or.

After his great victory in the European Championship he was the favourite. But he knew things could go wrong. He could still lose. He hates losing – like when his little brother beat him at croquet one summer day on Fitjar many, many years ago. Geir was so angry that he attacked his brother with the croquet mallet. It would probably not be a good idea to take that with him to Lyon.

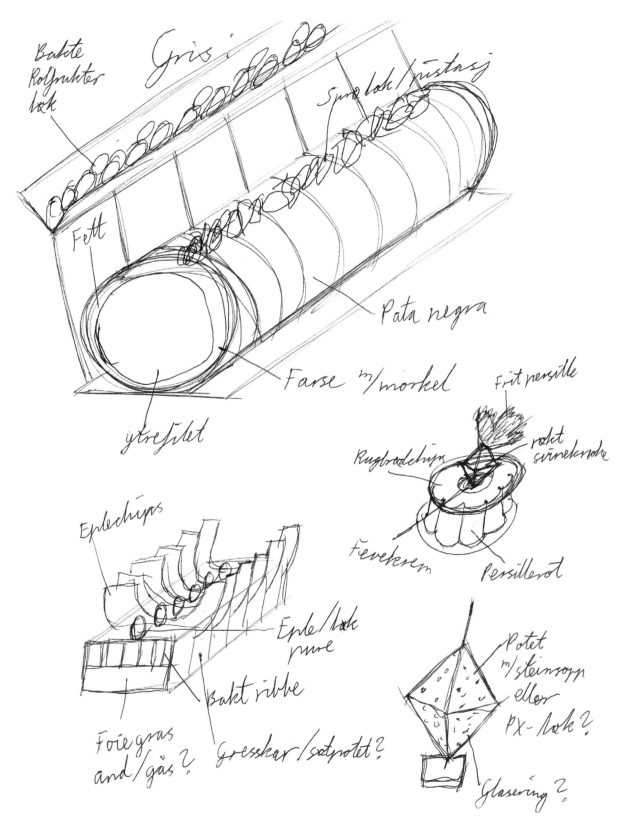

Sketches for "Chef of the Year" 2007.

CHEF OF THE YEAR 2007
WON WITH BURNT SAUCE

Geir's road to stardom started with his victory in the Norwegian Championship in 2003. That was when he got into the national team and was chosen to take part in "Chef of the Year" – The real qualifier for the Bocuse d'Or. Geir thinks it didn't actually go that well. He burnt the sauce for the arctic char and he wasn't satisfied with some of the dishes. But all the same, he won gold! And that meant he became the Norwegian contestant for the Bocuse d'Or.

ARCTIC CHAR "TARRAGON"

Geir's winning menu from "Chef of the Year" 2007.

Arctic char with tarragon stuffed with a tartare of lightly smoked arctic char

Polenta and truffle lasagne, three kinds of celery, avocado and pine nut ring with baby carrots, lobster in "nage-gelé" with fennel, spring onion and quail's eggs

Flavoured foam

"GRANDMA'S" PORK

Braised ribs of pork, foie gras and marinated sweet potato, topped with apples and spice caramel

Parsley root, broad beans and toasted rye bread with smoked pork

"Potato cubes PX" glazed with mustard seeds and dill

Poached and glazed sirloin with pata negra ham, crisp crackling, roasted root vegetables and leeks

Grandma's pork sauce and Riesling foam

143

HOW TO COAT BEFORE FRYING:

1. First coat in flour, to hold the rice pudding bars together.

2. Next coat in egg white, to make them firm and crisp.

3. Then coat in puffed oats.

4. Now they are ready to fry.

HOW TO MAKE CARAMEL BUBBLES:

1. Make caramel by melting 200 g/7 oz sugar. Make a ring of aluminium foil. Dip it in the caramel when it has begun to cool.

2. Blow gently until you have a small bubble. This takes a bit of practice.

3. Oops ... not too big!

4. Pull the bubble out so it gets a "stalk".

CLOUDBERRIES AND MORE CLOUDBERRIES

CLOUDBERRY AND ANIS SORBET:
150 g 150 ml/5 fl oz water
150 g//5½ oz sugar
2 star anis, crushed
400 g/14 oz cloudberries
50 ml/2 fl oz Lakka (cloudberry liqueur)
lemon juice

CLOUDBERRY CONSOMMÉ:
400 g/14 oz cloudberries
150 g/5½ oz sugar
400 g 400 ml/14 fl oz water

CLOUDBERRY AND MASCARPONE SOUFFLÉ:
800 g/1 lb 12 oz cloudberries
400 g/14 oz sugar
150 g/5½ oz mascarpone
300 g/10½ oz cream
5 gelatine leaves

BASIL JELLY:
1 bunch basil
300 ml/10 fl oz water
100 g//3½ oz sugar
3 gelatine leaves
1 lemon

FRIED RICE PUDDING:
200 ml/7 fl oz rise porridge
(firm, preferably with vanilla)
50 g/1¾ oz mascarpone
50 g/1¾ oz icing sugar
puffed oats
1 egg white
plain flour
1 litre neutral oil for frying

JOCONDE:
40 g/1½ oz icing sugar
40 g/1½ oz egg whites
40 g/1½ oz butter
60 g/2 oz flour
cocoa

CLOUDBERRY AND ANIS SORBET:
Boil the sugar and anis in water for 1 minute. Set aside to draw for 30 minutes. Remove the anis, add the cloud berries and bring to the boil again. Whiz in a blender, strain and flavour with lemon juice, Lakka and, if necessary, sugar. Stir and freeze in an ice cream maker.

CLOUDBERRY CONSOMME:
Boil all the ingredients for 2 minutes. Blend with a handblender and strain. Leave to cool.

CLOUDBERRY AND MASCARPONE SOUFFLÉ:
Boil the cloudberries and sugar for 5 minutes, mix and strain through a fine-mesh sieve. Soak the gelatine for 10 minutes. whip the cream until stiff and refrigerate. Mix the mascarpone into 450 g/1 lb of the cloudberry coulis and add the gelatine which will dissolve in it. Refrigerate until it has the desired consistency, mix in the cream and adjust the flavour with Lakka and lemon juice.

BASIL JELLY:
Soak the gelatine for 10 minutes. Bring the sugar and water to the boil. Cool and whiz in a blender with the basil until bright green. Strain through a fine-mesh sieve, add the dissolved gelatine and flavour with lemon juice. Pour the jelly into a flat-bottomed, straight-sided container to a depth of 3–4 mm/1/8 inch. After about 4 hours, when the jelly has set, cut in 5 mm/¼ inch cubes.

FRIED RICE PUDDING:
Mix together the rice porridge, mascarpone and icing sugar. Freeze in a rectangular mould lined with plastic film to give a layer 2 cm/¾ inch thick. Cut in bars of 8 x 2 cm/3¼ x ¾ inch. When it is frozen, coat in flour, then in beaten egg white and finally in roughly chopped puffed oats. Fry until golden at 180 °C/350 °F just before serving (must be warm all through; check by inserting a pointed knife).

JOCONDE:
Melt the butter, whisk in the egg whites and add the flour and sugar. Take 1 tablespoon of this mixture and mix with the cocoa. Spread a thin layer of the cocoa mixture on a silicone baking mat in a pattern of your choice and spread the pale mixture on top of it. Bake for 6 minutes at 120 °C/250 °F. Cut in strips about the height of the mould you are going to bake the soufflé in. You should do this while the joconde is warm. Line the soufflé moulds with the joconde, with the coloured patterns against the sides of the moulds. Pour in the soufflé mixture and freeze. Unmould and leave to thaw for 30 minutes before serving.

WINE TIPS
This dessert consists of cloudberries served in all kinds of different ways, with some spices and herbs and a little fat in the cream and creamed rice. A Malvasia from Lipari in Italy is very good, but a bit difficult to get hold of. It has an elegant freshness, but is made from dried grapes, which give it enough sweetness. Recioto from Soave in northern Italy is a little easier to get hold of and has a similar character.

Steeping clipfish

Put the fish in water for 3 days, changing the water each day.
Then steep for one day in milk, to give whiter fish.

CLIPFISH (DRIED, SALTED COD)

CLIPFISH:
200 g/7 oz clipfish, steeped
100 ml/3½ fl oz good quality olive oil
1 clove garlic
peel of 1 lemon, without the white pith
1 tsp fennel seeds

FENNEL + CREAM:
1 fennel bulb
2 tbsp good quality olive oil
½ tsp fennel seeds
1 tsp mashed potato powder

GAZPACHO:
100 ml/3½ fl oz gazpacho (see page 123)
1 leaf gelatine

POTATO CRISPS:
1 almond potato
50 ml/2 fl oz neutral oil for frying
salt and pepper

GARNISH:
1 celery
12 nice black olives (kalamata)

CLIPFISH:

Heat all the ingredients except for the fish in the oil. Set aside to draw for 15 minutes. Add the clipfish, making sure it is covered by the oil. Simmer at 80–90 °C/175–195 °F for 15 minutes. The fish should flake when pressed.

FENNEL:

Discard the first two layers of the fennel bulb. Cut the next layer in 12 thin sticks. Boil for 3 minutes in lightly salted water and cool in iced water. Cut the remainder of the fennel in small pieces and sauté with the oil and fennel seeds for 3 minutes. Add 100 ml/3½ fl oz water and cover. Cook the fennel until tender. This takes about 7–8 minutes. Evaporate all the water. Whiz the fennel in a blender to a smooth cream, add the mashed potato powder and mix well. The powder will give the purée a slightly firmer consistency, but will not affect the taste. Season with salt and pepper.

POTATO CRISPS:

Cut the potato in thin slices on a mandolin. Put them in cold water for 10 minutes to get rid of some of the starch. That makes it easier to get golden crisps without burning. Fry at 160 °C/320 °F until the oil stops bubbling and the potatoes are crisp. Transfer the crisps to a sheet of parchment and sprinkle with salt and pepper.

GARNISH:

Cut the celery in slices and boil for 1 minute, then cool in iced water. Slice the olives.

SERVING:

Heat up the gazpacho with the softened gelatine and then cool.

Split the fish into natural flakes. Pile all the ingredients up on the plates like a salad. Mash the gazpacho jelly with a spoon and arrange around the "salad" like a dressing. Lastly drizzle with the oil in which the fish was poached. This dish should be served warm.

HOW TO MAKE GAZPACHO JELLY:

1. Soak the gelatine in ice cold water for at least 5 minutes.

2. Add the softened gelatine to the gazpacho soup.

3. Pour the jelly mixture into a mould of your choice. Refrigerate for at least four hours.

WINE TIPS

Salt clipfish plus tomatoes and fennel are the main flavours here, with not much fat, just a little olive oil. Full-bodied Kerner wines from northern Italy take care of the acid, salt and the taste of the clipfish.

"I used lobster stock in this dish and burnt it during the competition."

ARCTIC CHAR WITH CRAYFISH *A LA NAGE*

ARCTIC CHAR:
1 piece arctic char, 0.8–1 kg/1 lb 12 oz–2 lb 4 oz
1 tsp chopped tarragon
4 thin slices bread
salt
1 tbsp butter
1 tbsp neutral oil

BOUILLON A LA NAGE:
4 large crayfish, each at least 150 g/3½ oz
400 ml/14 fl oz stock made from the crayfish shells (see page 186)
3 tbsp butter
2 tbsp good quality olive oil
lemon juice
salt
1 tsp tarragon, finely chopped

AVOCADO CREAM:
2 avocados
1 tsp coriander, finely chopped
1 lime
1 cm red chilli, finely chopped
½ clove garlic, finely chopped
2 tbsp good quality olive oil
salt and black pepper

VEGETABLES:
½ fennel
½ stick celery
8 spring carrots
50 g celeriac

ARCTIC CHAR:
Fillet the arctic char, remove the bones and skin and salt lightly. Cut in 4 portions. Sprinkle the skin side with finely chopped tarragon and cover with the bread. Fry in a hot pan with a little oil until half the fish has gone pale. Add the butter, remove from the heat and turn the fish. Let it lie for 10 seconds before serving.

A LA NAGE BOUILLON AND CRAYFISH:
Remove the tails from the crayfish and pull out the gut. Freeze the crayfish on a tray. They will keep for 6 months in the freezer in an airtight container or bag. When you want to use them, take them out and put them in a container of lukewarm water. Peel as for prawns. Bring the crayfish stock to the boil with the butter and olive oil. Mix with a hand mixed and season with salt and lemon juice. Cut each of the crayfish in 3 pieces and poach in the bouillon just before serving. Take out when ready, after 3–4 minutes.
It is important to stir the bouillon with a hand mixer just before serving to make sure it is smooth. Add the finely chopped tarragon.

AVOCADO CREAM:
Mash the avocado in a bowl with a whisk. Add the coriander, chilli and garlic together with the grated zest and juice of the lime. Beat in the olive oil and season with salt and pepper. Keep tightly covered with plastic film to prevent it from going brown. (It is oxidation that makes avocados turn brown, so exclude oxygen as far as possible.) The mixture can also be kept in a piping bag.

VEGETABLES:
Cut the vegetables in smallish pieces and simmer in the bouillon.

WINE TIPS

This is an elegant fish with not much fat, but we must take into account the fat in the avocado and bouillon and the sweetness from the crayfish. White Rhône wines from Hermitage or Condrieu are very suitable, as these wines have the oaky note that counteracts the fried bread and the butter in the bouillon, while having the tartness to match the fat. These wines are also sufficiently full-bodied to cope with the taste of the fish.

"Skyr is an Icelandic speciality, as this was a competition in which the main ingredients for the dishes were to come from Iceland. Skimmed milk yoghurt is an equivalent to skyr."

BLUEBERRY SOUFFLÉ

SOUFFLÉ:
200 g/7 oz blueberries/blackcurrants
10 g/¼ oz cornflour
50 g/1¾ oz sugar
200 g/7 oz egg whites
90 g/3¼ oz icing sugar
50 g/1¾ oz white chocolate, roughly chopped

CHIBOUST:
150 ml/5 fl oz cream
2 egg yolks
1 gelatine leaf
30 g/1 oz sugar
125 g/5¾ oz milk chocolate
150 ml/5 fl oz skyr/skimmed milk yoghurt

SORBET:
200 g/7 oz blueberries/blackcurrants
200 ml/7 fl oz water
200 ml/7 fl oz skyr/skimmed milk yoghurt
100 g/3½ oz sugar

SOUFFLÉ:
Bring the blueberries and sugar to the boil and mash with a hand mixer. Mix the cornflour in a little water, mix with the blueberries and boil for 2 minutes.

Whisk the egg whites to a meringue by hand (this is to get small bubbles in the meringue, which will make the soufflé more stable). Add the icing sugar when the egg whites are airy and whisk until the egg begins to shine and has a firm consistency. Grease soufflé moulds with butter and sprinkle with sugar. Stir the meringue into the blueberry mixture, add the white chocolate and spoon into the soufflé moulds. Level off the tops of the moulds and bake at 180 °C/350 °F for about 8–10 minutes. The soufflés should be just golden on top. Serve immediately. It is all right to open the oven door during cooking to check and turn the soufflés; it won't do any harm.

CHIBOUST:
Beat together 100 ml/3½ fl oz cream and skyr and refrigerate. Soak the gelatine. Mix the egg yolks, sugar and 50 ml/2 fl oz cream, and bring gently to the boil, stirring continuously. It can just bubble but no more, otherwise it will split. Then add the white chocolate and the softened gelatine. Let it melt for 1 minute before mixing so that it will become smooth. Cool to 37 °C/99 °F and fold in the whipped cream. Pour into a mould of your choice and chill for at least 3 hours before cutting into suitable portions if desired.

SORBET:
Bring the berries, water and sugar to the boil and purée with a hand mixer until smooth. Chill to a maximum of 20 °C/68 °F and add the skyr. Churn to a sorbet and freeze in an ice cream maker.

WINE TIPS

Here we have light berry flavours in the soufflé and sorbet, accompanied by a light chocolate cream. There is quite a high level of sweetness, so I would recommend a Riesling Beerenauslese or Trockenbeeren-auslese from the Mosel region of Germany. These wines have the fruity acid needed to counterbalance the blueberry sorbet.

HOW TO MAKE A SOUFFLÉ:

1. Whisk the egg whites and sugar in a big bowl. Beat until the consistency is airy and quite firm.

2. Add the icing sugar and continue whisking.

3. Fold the egg white mixture into the berries.

4. Add the pieces of chocolate.

Bent Stiansen was one of the judges for the Bocuse d'Or Europe. – Do you reckon he'll like the food?

BOCUSE D'OR EUROPE 2008
IN A CLASS OF HIS OWN

The training period for the Bocuse d´Or Europe
was hard, because Geir had a full-time job at
Midtåsen in Sandefjord. Nonethelees, it
exceeded all expectations. Geir himself thinks it's
the best he's done in any competition. He was a
great success with the judges and scored 50
points more than his nearest rival. It was
absolutely sensational!

SALMON "AUSTEVOLL"

Geir's winning menu for the Bocuse d'Or Europe.
The recipes on the following pages are a simplified version of
the dishes from this winning menu.

Cauliflower couscous filled with
salmon roe and covered with
broccoli stalks and green squash,
crisp cauliflower topping

Asparagus charlotte filled
with fried asparagus, morels
and asparagus cream

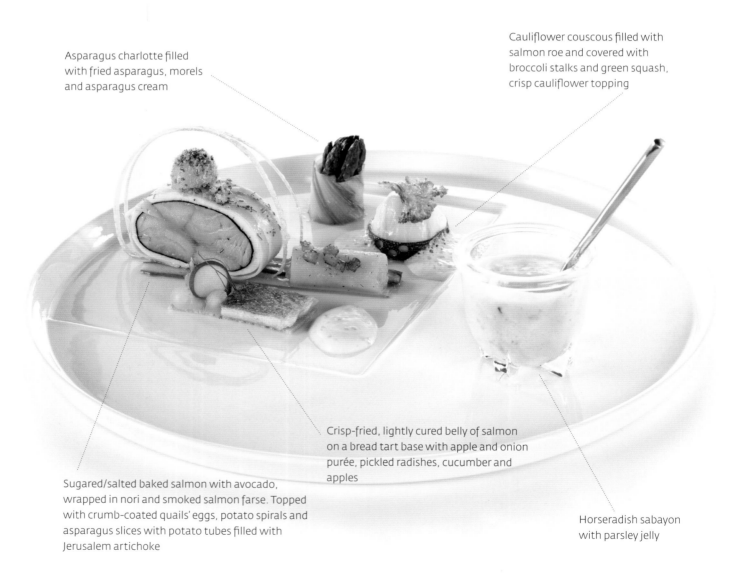

Crisp-fried, lightly cured belly of salmon
on a bread tart base with apple and onion
purée, pickled radishes, cucumber and
apples

Sugared/salted baked salmon with avocado,
wrapped in nori and smoked salmon farse. Topped
with crumb-coated quails' eggs, potato spirals and
asparagus slices with potato tubes filled with
Jerusalem artichoke

Horseradish sabayon
with parsley jelly

LAMB "FITJAR"

Glazed potato cubes with creamed ceps

Crisp-fried lambs' kidneys with mustard, on skewers with glazed red onions and onion crisps

Roast flank of lamb with rillette of lamb shank and apricots.

Glazed sweetbread and lamb sausage with mustard seeds

Rolled sirloin and tenderloin of lamb with root vegetables flavoured with mustard and tarragon wrapped in leg of lamb and glazed

Radish "agnolotti" filled with summer cabbage flavoured with salsa verde

Artichoke slices and creamed artichoke topped with summer vegetables (broad beans, carrots, turnips)

SALMON "AUSTEVOLL"

SALMON "AUSTEVOLL"

SALMON x 2:
1 kg/2 lb 4 oz salmon fillets
with skin
15 g/¼ oz salt
10 g/¼ oz sugar
3 nori leaves (sushi seaweed)
grated zest of ½ lemon
1 tbsp dill, chopped

HORSERADISH SABAYON:
2 egg whites
1 tsp Dijon mustard
200 g7 oz butter
250 ml/8 floz dry Riesling
2 shallots
2 tsp grated horseradish

**CAULIFLOWER AND
MORELS:**
¼ cauliflower
100 g/3½ oz morels
1 shallot
1 tbsp butter

4 quail's eggs

MARINATED VEGETABLES:
1 tart apple
2 radishes
4 small onions
½ cucumber
1 tsp grated horseradish
4 tbsp apple vinegar
2 tbsp sugar
2 tbsp water
lemon juice
2 tbsp salmon roe
1 sprig dill

ASPARAGUS AND OIL:
12 asparagus
50 ml/2 fl oz neutral oil
salt flakes
zest of ½ lemon
pepper

PARSLEY/HORSERADISH JELLY:
50 ml/3 tbsp water
3 sprigs parsley
zest of ½ lemon
1 tsp grated horseradish
1 gram agar agar

HOW TO MAKE SABAYON:

1. Boil (reduce) wine and onion by half in a saucepan. Melt butter in another saucepan.

2. Beat eggs and mustard for 2–3 minutes until airy. Add the wine mixture to the egg and mustard mixture. Stir gently together.

3. Add melted butter in a thin stream, whisking hard all the time. It is important that the butter should be at exactly the same temperature as the mixture, about 50 °C/120 °F. Otherwise the sauce may split.

SALMON x 2:

Scrape the scales off the salmon fillets and cut off the skin together with 1 cm flesh all over. Salt and sugar the flesh on the skin and the fillets. Sprinkle the meat on the skin with dill. Refrigerate for 2 hours. Cut the salmon fillets lengthways and lay one part of each on top of the other to give a kind of long sausage. Roll tightly in nori and plastic film. Bake the fish at 50 °C/120 °F until the internal temperature reaches 43 °C/109 °F and let it rest for 5 minutes before serving. Cut the salmon skin in pieces 8 x 10 cm/3¼ x 4 inches and fry on the skin side over high heat, pressing down slightly. They should be half-cooked and the skin should be crisp. This must be done immediately before serving. Cut in two and turn up the edges. Arrange the marinated vegetables on top.

MARINATED VEGETABLES:

Boil the onion in water until tender. Peel the cucumber, remove the seeds and cut in pieces 1 cm/½ inch thick. Mix the sugar, vinegar and water and pour over the cucumber and onion. Cut the radishes in narrow wedges and marinate with the other vegetables. Cut the apple in thin strips and drizzle with a little lemon juice to prevent browning. Serve with salmon roe and dill.

SABAYON:

Reduce the shallot in Riesling by half and purée smooth with a hand mixer. Melt the butter completely until it stops bubbling, so the salt and milk proteins will sink to the bottom of the pan. Whisk the egg whites until airy in a bowl over a saucepan of boiling water. You will have to adjust the bowl a little occasionally so that the egg whites do not coagulate and form lumps. When the egg whites are airy, add the mustard and horseradish. Continue whisking and add 3 tablespoons of the reduced Riesling. Continue whisking over the heat. The temperature should be just above body temperature. Add the butter, which should now be at about 50 °C/122 °F. If desired, adjust the flavour by adding a little more

reduced Riesling. Serve the sauce now or transfer it to a siphon with a gas cartridge. If you keep the sauce at about 50 °C/122 °F now, it will keep for 5–6 hours. Spray out when serving. This produces a very airy sabayon. I don't use egg yolks in this sauce in order to make it fresher and lighter. (You can also make a jelly of parsley and horseradish puréed with water and lemon peel, based on agar or carrageenan jelly. These can tolerate heat. When they have set, crush them with a spoon and mix into the sabayon. That will produce "explosions of flavour" inside the sabayon.)

ASPARAGUS AND OIL:

Peel only the bottom part of the asparagus and make asparagus soup from the peel (same method as for herb oil, see page 163). Cook the asparagus al dente before serving and dress with the asparagus oil, a little lemon peel, salt and pepper.

CAULIFLOWER AND MORELS:

Divide the cauliflower into small florets. Slice the onion. Cut up the morels, making sure to remove all the sand. Sauté the onion and morels in the butter, add the cauliflower florets and sauté for 2–3 minutes. The cauliflower should be al dente. Season with salt and pepper. Serve with poached quail eggs on top of the fish.

WINE TIPS

Here we have the oily salmon together with the light green tones of the asparagus, the slightly earthy note of the morels, and the tartness of the vegetables. The slight acidity and body of a Pouilly Fumé from the Loire might be suitable. However the best choice would be a wine from Central Burgundy, which has an oaky note to counterbalance the morels but also has enough acid and body to match the sauce and vegetables. Slightly older top-quality Chablis also works well.

HOW TO POACH AN EGG:

1. Break the egg into a bowl and pour in vinegar. Shake the bowl a little and add 1 tablespoon water. Leave to stand for 10 minutes until the inner part of the egg white becomes whiter and firmer.

2. Strain off the thin outer part of the white.

3. Bring the water to the boil and remove the pan from the heat. Stir the water so that it rotates.

4. Put the egg into the rotating water and simmer for 3 minutes. Poached eggs may be kept in salt water in the refrigerator for a few days if you want to store them.

LAMB "FITJAR"

LAMB "FITJAR"

LAMB FILLET:
800 g/1 lb 12 oz fillet of lamb with fat
1 sprig tarragon
2 tbsp butter
salt and pepper

BAKED FLANK:
1 flank of lamb
salt and pepper
3 cloves garlic
1 tsp fennel seeds
500 ml/18 fl oz neutral oil

ARTICHOKES:
2 artichokes
3 tbsp good quality olive oil
1 lemon
½ carrot
½ onion
salt
50 g/1¾ oz celeriac
1 sprig parsley

SALSA VERDE:
1 sprig parsley
1 tsp Dijon mustard
50 ml/2 fl oz good quality olive oil
20 g/¾ oz spinach
grated zest of ¼ lemon
20 g/¾ oz parmesan

PARSLEY OIL:
50 g/1¾ oz parsley
200 ml/7 fl oz neutral oil
grated zest of ½ lemon

CREAMED POTATO:
500 g/1 lb 2 oz almond potatoes
2 tbsp Dijon mustard
2 tbsp tarragon, finely chopped
2 tbsp butter
1 dl cream
salt and pepper

LAMB GRAVY:
200 ml/7 fl oz reduced beef stock
300 ml/10 fl oz reduced lamb stock
50 ml/2 fl oz dry white wine
1 shallot, chopped
1 clove garlic
1 sprig tarragon
3 tbsp butter
salt and pepper
lemon juice

VEGETABLES:
12 small carrots
4 turnips
4 small red onions
1 lemon
200 g broad beans, or peas
½ spring cabbage
2 tbsp sugar
2 tbsp butter
salt and pepper

HOW TO PREPARE ARTICHOKES:

1. Cut off the stalk.

2. Cut off all the leaves.

3. Cut off the outermost layer around the artichoke heart, until that is all you have left of the artichoke.

4. Cut off the top of the flower.

5. Trim around the heart – all the green must go.

6. Trim the top of the artichoke.

7. Scoop out the hairs with a spoon.

8. Finished!

BAKED FLANK:

Salt and pepper the flank lightly and roll up. Wrap the roll in a cloth and tie firmly with string. Lay the roll in the oil with all the flavourings and garlic. Bake in the oven at 90 °C/195 °F for 6 hours. Cool, remove from the cloth and tie with string again, to prevent it from opening. Fry on all sides in a pan with a little oil. Before serving warm up in the oven at 150 °C/300 °F for 8 minutes. Cut the meat in slices when it is hot.

ARTICHOKES:

Cut all the vegetables apart from the lemon and artichokes in small pieces. Put in a pan with water and olive oil so they are just covered. Bring to the boil, simmer for 20 minutes, then add the grated lemon zest and lemon juice. Season with salt. Prepare the artichokes as shown in the pictures. Add them to the other vegetables so they are covered by the liquid. Cover with a sheet of baking parchment to keep out the air. Simmer over low heat for 20–30 minutes. Check if they are tender by sticking a knife in them. Cool in the liquid. Cut in cakes and heat up in a little of the liquid.

SALSA VERDE:

Freeze the olive oil for 30 minutes. Put all the other ingredients in a small blender and add the oil. Whiz to a smooth cream. We freeze the oil to make the cream homogenous. If it isn't frozen, the salsa will split. Salsa will for a week in the refrigerator in an airtight container.

PARSLEY OIL:

Whiz the parsley, oil and lemon peel in a blender for 3 minutes. Bring to the boil, strain through a fine-meshed sieve and refrigerate. This is the standard method for herb oils and can be used for any herbs.

CREAMED POTATO:

Peel the potatoes and boil until tender. Drain and mash immediately. It is important to do this straight away to avoid getting lumps in the mash. Add the cream, butter, mustard and tarragon and season with salt and pepper. Keep warm until serving. If you let it cool and warm it up again, creamed potato will be less airy.

LAMB GRAVY:

Sauté the onion with little tarragon until transparent. Pour over the wine and reduce completely. Add the beef and lamb stock and boil for 10 minutes. Strain and season with salt, pepper and lemon juice. Whisk in the butter and add finely chopped tarragon just before serving. I use both lamb and beef stock in lamb gravy, because pure lamb gravy has a slightly sharp taste, so I give it a rounder flavour with beef stock.

LAMB FILLET:

Fry the fillets on the fat side until golden and crisp. Turn the meat and remove from the heat while you add the butter and tarragon. Season with salt and pepper. I add the salt and pepper after frying, because the salt draws out the moisture, which prevents the meat from forming the crust that gives it the nice flavour (resulting from the Maillard reaction, similar to caramellisation). This is of no importance for retaining the juices in the meat, but rather the opposite. More moisture is lost by browning the meat first than by putting it straight in the oven. Roast the fillets in the oven for 8–10 minutes at 190 °C/375 °F. The internal temperature should be 54–55 °C/129–131 °F when you take them out. Allow to rest for 10 minutes and cut into 4 portions.

VEGETABLES:

Boil the carrots with the skins on for 2 minutes and cool in iced water. Now you will be able to pull off the skin with your fingers. Peel the turnips, cut in wedges, blanch in lightly salted water for 1 minute and cool in iced water. Turnips are best when they are almost raw. If they are well done, they don't taste good. Shell the broad beans, boil in water for 2 minutes, cool in iced water and remove from their skins. Boil the red onion in water for 5 minutes, then put in a saucepan with lemon juice, lemon peel and sugar. Glaze with this before serving. Warm up the turnips, broad beans and carrots with a little butter and salt before serving. Cut the cabbage in thin strips and Heat in a saucepan with a little water and butter. Drain and toss in 3 tablespoons salsa verde and season with salt and pepper.

WINE TIPS

A very good accompaniment to the light summer flavours of lamb and lamb gravy is a Pinot Noir from either Burgundy or New Zealand. The acidity will help to counterbalance the fat in the lamb and the fruitiness goes well with the vegetables and sauce.

Meat tips:

I add salt and pepper after roasting, because the salt draws out the moisture that prevents the meat from getting the crisp outside that gives it the lovely flavour (which comes from caramelising, the maillard process). It is of no importance for keeping the juices in the meat – quite the contrary. More moisture is lost by browning the meat first than by putting it straight into the oven.

"Cod can be used in many ways, because it can go with lots of different flavours. Norwegian cod in the winter is one of the nicest things I know."

THE MOMENT OF TRUTH

It was 6 o'clock in the evening. The winter sky was dark over Lyon. Geir had served the last culinary work of art to the judges at two in the afternoon. Ever since then he had been waiting.

Everything was timed down to the last second. Five hours, 18,000 seconds, tick-tock, now the fish dish must be ready. Tick-tock, now it's time to present the meat. Tick-tock, is the onion pyramid ready? Now and then he glanced up, looked at all the Norwegian flags, let the shouting, cheering and fanfares of trumpets sneak into his ears and out again. Focus. FOCUS. The pieces of black truffle must be perfectly square ... must check the cod that's baking in the oven ... that the prawn is exactly in the middle of the cube of aspic ... that the tips of the puff pastry round the fillet of beef are even ... the oven timer rings, quick, quick, where's the brandade?

Geir was the first chef out when the competition started early this morning. He had waited longest. For the verdict on his dream. Rumours had been circulating about overcooked scallops, sauces that were too salty, poorly executed garnishes, bad timing. And about the Frenchman's meat dish that fell apart. Could it be true? He was one of the favourites, wasn't he?

President Hellstrøm turned and smiled as he stood with the Norwegian flag right in front of Geir. All the 24 teams had just marched into the arena, exactly like the Olympic Games, row upon row of white chefs' hats. But should Eyvind really have been smiling? Rumour had it that the Nordic countries had done well, but which of the Nordic countries?

Geir could still feel the irritation in his stomach – about the puff pastry that wasn't the right shape, the herb oil he forgot when he was serving the beef, and the horseradish sauce that should have been seasoned better ... But might it be enough? Might it???

The consolation prizes were announced first. The most attractive posters and similar trivialities. Then the best meat and the best fish after the medallists. The poor Dane. He got best meat. Geir couldn't understand it; after all, the Dane was one of the very best. He looked pretty disappointed too. Suppose Norway was announced as best fish? Geir's heartbeats drowned out the noise of the audience. Don't say Norvège, not now, not yet! Phew! Denmark again. The poor Dane.

The tension mounted. Geir had a forest of French flags in front of him. Suddenly they stopped waving, because France, the land of gourmet food, was awarded bronze. No Marseillaise. No honour. The defeat was almost as great as when Napoleon lost to the Russians. Suddenly all the French press photographers disappeared – in the middle of the award ceremony – there was nothing else to take pictures of.

Silver for Sweden. Now there was only one medal left. Geir wiped his brow with his hand. His skin was clammy. He took a deep breath as the legendary chef Paul Bocuse took the microphone. Geir could see the old man's lips moving, but he couldn't hear what country he said. There was too much noise.

But Hellstrøm heard it, and Hellstrøm leapt high in the air, as if he was trying to win the high jump, and the Norwegians in the audience suddenly shouted much louder than all the others. Red, white and blue. Geir looked at all the flags and realises what's happened. Gold! He had won gold in the Bocuse d'Or.

He ran over to Solvold and gave him a hug. The champagne sprayed. Katrine came running towards him. He had never seen her looking so happy. The press photographers came running, everybody came running. Someone handed him a mobile phone. Suddenly he was in direct contact with the news programme Dagsrevyen, trying to put a few words together, trying to explain how he felt. In a brief flashback he sees the 13-year-old watching a television cookery programme and resolving to become world champion. It's surreal. It's TRUE. Geir isn't in the habit of laughing, but now he can't hold back the tears.

This one chance. This one dream. About this very moment.

A happy young man on the winner's rostrum. Silver to the Swede Jonas Lundgren, bronze to the Frenchman Philippe Mille.

"It was my own personal D-day, when everything had to go right,
from the heating cables in the hotplate dish, to the consistency
of the sabayon. I have never been so nervous or so happy."

BOCUSE D'OR 2009
A HISTORIC VICTORY

On the world map of fine food,
Norway is a small country. But we
have never been as great as during
the Bocuse d'Or in 2009. It wasn't
just the fact that Geir won. He won with
24 points more than the Swede who came
second. No-one has ever won the
Bocuse d'Or so convincingly before!

COD AND SCALLOPS "SANDEFJORD"

Geir's winning menu for the Bocuse d'Or.
The recipes on the following pages are a simplified version of
the dishes from this winning menu.

POTATOES AND LEEKS
Tubes of potato filled with leek
and potato cream, with coated,
fried almond potatoes topped
with poached quail's eggs

BEETROOT CUBE
Baked beetroot filled with
baked Jerusalem artichokes
and truffles

PRAWNS "CABARET"
Prawn jelly with boiled prawns, prawn
mousse filled with baked celery and
topped with raw prawn carpaccio,
peas and baby onions and prawn foam

SPICE-BAKED LOIN OF COD
in a bread crust, with sweet potato
flakes with brandade roll, green
pea sphere with bacon, lightly
smoked scallops and belly of cod
topped with olive cream

Sabayon sauce with Riesling and
parsley jelly

BEEF "SÆTERBØ"

Browned onions on onion jelly with browned onions inside

Potato and truffle cream with bone marrow

Parsley root and suede charlotte with spinach cream and glazed beef cheek with duck liver

Tenderloin with black truffles and lardons, turnips in a red wine glaze and carved mushrooms, puff pastry

Beef chops with parsley and garlic, fried duck liver and artichokes. Crispy onions, crisp beef fat, fried breadcrumb crust.

Oxtail terrine with raisins and onions, celery root and leeks, apple crisps

Asparagus beans, carrots, roasted garlic, artichokes and ravioli with artichoke and truffle cream. Truffle foam

Red wine and bay-leaf gravy

WINE TIPS

This dish has delicate flavours: peas, scallops and prawns (with a little smokiness). The strongest flavour is that of the fried scallops. Try a dry Riesling from good vineyards in the Rheingau, a wine which has a slight mineral note, as well as the acidity and body to match the fried scallops without overpowering the prawns. There is quite a lot of sweetness in shellfish, and the fruitiness of the Riesling works well to counterbalance this.

SCALLOPS "SANDEFJORD"

PRAWN FOAM:
200 ml/7 fl oz raw prawn stock (for shellfish stock see page 186)
200 ml/7 fl oz cream
½ lemon

PEA PURÉE:
200 g/7 oz frozen peas
50 ml/2 fl oz chicken stock
1 shallot, chopped
2 tbsp butter
salt and pepper
50 g/1¾ oz fresh peas

SWEET POTATO:
1 sweet potato
salt and pepper

SMOKED PRAWNS:
100 g/3½ oz cooked prawns, rinsed
2 tbsp wood chips for smoking

SCALLOPS:
4 large fresh scallops
1 tbsp neutral oil
salt and pepper
1 tbsp butter

4 poached quail's eggs (see page 159)
pea sprouts

PRAWN FOAM:

Bring the prawn stock and cream to the boil and simmer for 10 minutes. Grate in some lemon zest and season with lemon juice, salt and pepper. Foam with a hand mixer before serving.

PEA PURÉE:

Sauté the shallot in butter until transparent. Add the frozen peas and chicken stock (may be replaced by water). Cover and boil for 3 minutes. Strain off the liquid and whiz in a blender with the butter to a smooth purée. Season with salt and pepper. Boil the fresh peas for 2 minutes and cool in iced water. Squeeze the flesh out of the pea shells. Warm the flesh in a little butter before serving and season with salt and pepper.

SWEET POTATOE:

Cut the sweet potato in thin slices with a food slicer or mandolin. Boil in lightly salted water until just tender and transfer to an oiled baking sheet. Heat up under the grill before serving.

SMOKED PRAWNS:

Peel the cooked prawns and smoke for 5 minutes in a portable smoker (obtainable from camping equipment shops). Warm up a little with the peas before serving.

SCALLOPS:

Fry the scallops on the long sides (not the short ends) in a smoking hot pan with a little oil. When they have turned nice and brown on that side, remove from the heat and add butter to the pan. Salt and pepper the scallops and pour over a little butter. It takes about 2–3 minutes to fry the scallops. It is important not to fry them for too long or they will go hard.

HOW TO FRY SCALLOPS:

Heat the frying pan until it smokes. Add a little oil. Put in the scallops and fry over high heat until they turn golden. When they are golden in colour, remove the pan from the heat. Add butter and turn the shellfish. Pour a little of the butter over them.

COD "SANDEFJORD"

COD "SANDEFJORD"

COD:
800 g/1 lb 12 oz cod
2 tsp salt

BOLLINIOS:
1 cod belly
50 g/1¾ oz clipfish
½ leek
1 tbsp butter
50 g/1¾ oz breadcrumbs
(fresh crumbs) or Panko
1 egg white
a little plain flour
1 clove garlic
½ boiled almond potato
2 slices bacon

HERB OIL:
2 tbsp fennel seeds
2 tbsp coriander seeds
grated zest of 1 lemon
4 cloves garlic
200 ml/7 fl oz good quality
olive oil
salt

CRUST:
50 g/1¾ oz butter
30 g/1 oz breadcrumbs
(fresh crumbs) or Panko
grated zest ¼ lemon
1 clove garlic

BAKED BEETROOT:
2 beetroot
lemon juice
salt and pepper

JERUSALEM ARTICHOKE
CREAM:
300 g/10½ oz Jerusalem
artichokes
100 ml/3½ fl oz milk
3 tbsp butter
2 tbsp mascarpone
salt and pepper
10 g/¼ oz black truffle
(may be omitted)

SABAYON:
2 egg whites
1 tsp Dijon mustard
200 g/7 oz butter
200 ml/7 fl oz dry Riesling
2 shallots

GRILLED LEEK:
8 cm/3¼ inches leek
(the bottom part)

WINE TIPS

There is a little fat in the accompaniments, along with the earthy notes of the truffles, Jerusalem artichokes and beetroot. There is also a slight nutty flavour from the browned butter in the topping on the fish. The wine that has the same characteristics is definitely Meursault, with a buttery flavour, nutty aroma, a high acid level to counterbalance the sabayon and the fat, and body and mineral notes for the cod.

GRILLED LEEK:

Cut the leek in 2 cm/¾ inch thick slices and grill. Transfer to a baking sheet and add a little of the oil from the fish, salt and pepper and cover with foil. Bake in the oven for 10 minutes at 150 °C/300 °F. May be cooled now and warmed up again before serving.

HERB OIL:

Put all the ingredients for the herb oil in a saucepan and bring to the boil. Simmer over low heat for 1 hour. Purée with a hand mixer and strain the oil. This oil will keep for a long time in the refrigerator.

COD:

Salt the cod and refrigerate.

BREAD CRUST:

Brown the butter for the bread topping with the garlic. Remove the garlic and let the butter cool. Mix together with the bread-crumbs and lemon zest. Spread the mixture on baking parchment, about 2 mm/1/8 inch thick, and put in the freezer. When it is hard, cut in squares of a suitable size to go with the pieces of fish. Keep in the refrigerator.

BOLLINIOS:

Salt the cod belly, cover with foil and bake in the oven with the garlic at 150 °C/300 °F for 10 minutes. Mix with ½ boiled almond potato and buttered leek. Season with grated clipfish. Roll into balls of 4–5 cm/1½–2 inches diameter and freeze. Fry the bacon until crisp, dry well and cut in small pieces. Whisk the egg white for 20 seconds. Dip the fish balls in plain flour, then in egg white and finally in a mixture of breadcrumbs and bacon. Fry at 180 °C/350 °F for 4–5 minutes before serving. Check that they are warmed through by sticking a knife in them.

BAKED BEETROOT:

Bake the beetroot in the oven, whole and in their skins at 180 °C/350 °F for about 1 hour. Check that they are tender all through. Allow to cool, remove the skin and cut in 2 cm/¾ inch cubes. Heat the cubes with a little olive oil and season with lemon juice, salt and pepper.

JERUSALEM ARTICHOKE CREAM:

Peel the Jerusalem artichoke and boil in water and milk until tender. This takes about 30 minutes. Drain off the water and dry the artichoke a little in the pan. Whiz in a blender with butter and mascarpone to a smooth cream. Season with salt, pepper and, if desired, flavour with grated black truffle.

SABAYON:

Boil the shallot and Riesling, reduce by half and purée with a hand mixer until smooth. Melt the butter until it stops bubbling, so the salt and milk proteins will sink to the bottom of the pan. Whisk the egg whites until airy in a bowl over a saucepan of boiling water. You will have to adjust the bowl a little occasionally so that the egg whites do not coagulate and form lumps. When it is airy, add the mustard. Continue whisking and add 3 tablespoons reduced Riesling. Continue whisking over heat; the temperature should be just above body temperature. Mix in the butter, which is now at about 50°C/120 °F. If desired, adjust the flavour by adding a little more reduced Riesling. Serve the sauce now or transfer it to a siphon with a gas cartridge. If you keep the sauce at about 50 °C/120 °F now, it will keep for 5–6 hours. Spray out when serving. This produces a very airy sabayon. I don't use egg yolks in this sauce in order to make it fresher and lighter.

COD:

Divide the cod into 4 portions and rub well with the herb oil. Cover with foil or with a lid and bake at 56 °C/135 °F for about 30 minutes or longer. It makes no difference if you leave it in for 1½ hours, because when the fish reaches 56 °C/133 °F it doesn't change. This is the best interior temperature for cod. Before serving, top with the breadcrumb mixture and put the fish under the grill for 1 minute to add a little extra heat and gratinate the topping.

WINE TIPS

Braised meat has a strong flavour and needs a powerful wine. Wines that work well are those from the northern part of the Rhône Valley, for example Côte-Rôtie, or Châteauneuf du Pape from the southern Rhône. These are juicy wines with plenty of strength to cope with the strong flavour of the meat.

ABERDEEN ANGUS BEEF "SÆTERBØ" 1

BEEF CHEEK:
1 beef cheek
500 ml/18 fl oz beef stock
½ tsp salt

OXTAIL TERRINE:
1 oxtail, boiled to make the beef stock
100 g/3½ oz raisins
1 shallot, sliced
100 ml/3½ fl oz dry Riesling
200 g/7 oz celeriac
salt and pepper
200 ml/7 floz reduced beef stock

MUSTARD FOAM:
50 ml/2 fl oz dry Riesling
1 shallot, chopped
200 ml/7 fl oz chicken stock
200 ml/7 fl oz cream
1 tbsp mustard
salt and pepper

GARNISH:
1 stick celery
½ celeriac
2 tbsp sour cream
½ kohl rabi
1 parsley root
50 g/1¾ oz spinach
1 shallot, sliced
1 tbsp butter
2 tbsp good quality olive oil

BEEF CHEEK:
Rinse the beef cheek thoroughly in running water. Put in a pan with the stock, cover and boil for 4 hours. In the competition I used a pressure cooker, and then it took 1½ hours. Leave to cool and cut in 2 cm/¾ inch cubes. Heat in the stock before serving. Bring the stock to the boil and foam well. Strain through a fine-meshed sieve and season with salt and pepper. You will use this bouillon later.

OX TAIL TERRINE:
Boil the raisins and onion in Riesling in a covered pan until the raisins are big and soft. Use the raisins in the terrine and the onion on top. Pull all the meat off the oxtail and put in a saucepan with the beef stock. Reduce. Cut the celeriac in 3–4 mm/¼ inch cubes. When there is very little liquid remaining, add the celeriac and cook until tender along with the meat. When all the liquid has boiled away, season with salt and pepper and add the raisins. Press into a mould lined with plastic film. It should be 2–3 cm/¾–1¼ inches thick. Refrigerate and cut in rectangles. Warm up gently before serving.

MUSTARD FOAM:
Sauté the onion until transparent and add the wine. Reduce completely. Add the chicken stock and boil for 5 minutes. Add the cream and boil for a further 5 minutes. Season the sauce with salt, pepper and mustard. Strain and foam up with a hand mixer before serving.

GARNISH:
Boil ¼ celeriac in water until tender and purée with the sour cream in a blender to a smooth cream. Season with salt and pepper. Cut the kohl rabi, the remainder of the celeriac and the parsley root in 2 cm/¾ inch cubes and boil in the oxtail bouillon until tender. Cut the celery in thin slices, blanch for 20 seconds and plunge in iced water. Dress the celery with olive oil, lemon juice, salt and pepper before serving.

Sauté the spinach and shallot in butter before serving. Serve all the elements hot: the bouillon, root vegetables, ox cheek and spinach in a bowl with mustard foam and the terrine topped with creamed celeriac, celery, a few raisins and some onion.

ABERDEEN ANGUS BEEF
"SÆTERBØ" 2

ABERDEEN ANGUS BEEF "SÆTERBØ" 2

BEEF:
800 g/1 lb 12 oz sirloin of beef (preferably Aberdeen Angus)
salt and pepper
2 tbsp butter
1 tbsp neutral oil

GREMOLATA:
1 sprig parsley
1 clove garlic
grated zest of 1 lemon
100 ml/3½ fl oz good quality olive oil

BROWNED ONIONS:
3 onions
4 tbsp butter
½ tsp salt
pepper
1 tsp sherry vinegar

VEGETABLES:
4 large white asparagus
½ lemon
1 tsp sugar
1 tsp salt
3 tbsp butter
12 small carrots
200 g/7 oz asparagus beans

FOIE GRAS:
4 x 50 g/1¾ oz slices of foie gras
salt and pepper

BAY leaf GRAVY:
300 ml/10 fl oz reduced beef stock
50 ml/2 fl oz red wine
4 bay leaves (fresh)
1 shallot
1 clove garlic
3 tbsp butter

GREMOLATA:
Whiz all the ingredients for the gremolata in a blender until smooth. Will keep for up to 1 week in the refrigerator.

BROWNED ONIONS:
Slice the onion and put in a pan with the butter and salt. Cook over low heat for 1–1½ hours, until the onion is golden. It is important that the heat should be low in order to get the right consistency and flavour. Season with vinegar, pepper and salt.

BAY GRAVY:
Sauté the onion until transparent and add the red wine and bay leaves. Reduce completely, add the beef stock and boil for 10 minutes. Strain the stock, season with salt and pepper and stir in the butter.

VEGETABLES:
Peel the white the asparagus all the way up. Bring 1 litre water to the boil with salt, sugar, lemon peel, lemon juice and butter. Add the asparagus and simmer over low heat for 10–15 minutes. It should be well done. White asparagus is not nice al dente. Boil the spring carrots first for 2 minutes, cool and pull off the skins. Boil the asparagus beans for 2 minutes and cool on iced water. Before serving, heat up all the vegetables in a saucepan with a little gremolata. Season with salt and pepper.

BEEF:
Divide the meat into 4 steaks and grill well in a grill pan. Rub the steaks with gremolata and season with salt and pepper. Roast at 160 °C/320 °F for about 10 minutes. The interior temperature should be 50 °C/122 °F when you take them out. Leave to rest for 10 minutes before serving.

FOIE GRAS:
Fry the foie gras in a dry pan over high heat for 1 minute on each side. Season with salt and pepper.

Arrange the onion under the meat with all the vegetables and the foie gras on top. Pour a little of the oil from the vegetables round the meat before adding the sauce.

WINE TIPS
A nice piece of medium rare roast beef and fine roasted root vegetables, served with sweetish onions and a nice, rich beef gravy. A good Mercurey works very well here. It is full-bodied enough to clean up the stronger flavours and the fat in the browned onions. Another good choice would be a strong Spanish wine from Ribera del Duero.

Champagne on the winner's podium!

SHELLFISH

1 kg/2 lb 4 oz shellfish shells, fresh. It is important to make the stock on the same day that the shells are cleaned out
100 ml/3½ fl oz neutral oil
1 carrot
¼ celeriac
2 onions
1 garlic bulb
1 fennel bulb
100 g/3½ oz canned tomatoes
1 tsp fennel seeds
1 tsp coriander seeds

Peel all the vegetables and cut in small pieces. The size of the vegetables depends on how long the stock is to cook for. Shellfish stock is boiled for 30 minutes, so the pieces should be small. Heat a wide saucepan and add the oil with the fennel and coriander seeds. Add the shells and crush well with a big wooden spoon. There is a slight difference between various types of shellfish. You should just fry raw prawns quickly for 1 minute before adding the vegetables, lobster/crab should be fried fiercely for at least 5 minutes, and scampi a little less fiercely for 3–4 minutes. Add the vegetables and tomatoes and fry a little longer. Add sufficient cold water to just cover the shellfish. It is important not to add too much water, because that gives a thin stock that will need to be reduces later, which diminishes the flavour. Bring the stock to the boil and simmer over low heat for 30 minutes (20 minutes for prawns). Shellfish stock shouldn't be skimmed, as that takes away a lot of the nice flavour. Strain. You can remove the oil that forms on top of the stock when it cools and use it as shellfish oil. If you want to make soup, you can replace the water with milk. Then you can just add a little butter or cream after straining and you will have a nice shellfish soup.

LAMB

5 kg/11 lb lamb bones
2 carrots
3 onions
1 garlic bulb
1 tbsp tomato purée
½ celeriac
½ leek
3 bay leaves
1 sprig rosemary
1 sprig thyme

Roast the lamb bones in the oven at 190 °C/375 °F for 1 hour. Cut up all the vegetables roughly and fry until golden in a saucepan with a little oil. Add the tomato purée and herbs and fry for a further 3 minutes. Add the bones. It is important to heat the oven tray with a little water, because there will be lots of nice flavour on it. Cover the bone well with water and bring to the boil. Skim and reduce the heat so it simmers. Cook for 4–5 hours. Strain and reduce.

BEEF

5 kg/11 lb oxtail
2 carrots
3 onions
1 garlic bulb
½ celeriac
½ leek
3 bay leaves
1 sprig rosemary
1 sprig thyme

Roast the oxtail in the oven at 200 °C/400 °F for 1 hour. Cut the onion in two and fry in a dry pan until black underneath, but not charred. Roughly chop all the other vegetables and put them in the pan with the oxtail, herbs and onion. Cover the meat well with water. Bring to the boil, skim and reduce the heat so it simmers. Cook for at least 6 hours. Strain and reduce. If stocks are cooked over low heat, it will not need to be skimmed during cooking or reducing, as long as they are strained afterwards. There is a lot of flavour in what you skim off.

CHICKEN

5 kg/11 lb chicken carcasses
3 carrots
3 onions
1 leek
1 garlic bulb
3 bay leaves
1 celeriac
1 sprig parsley

Rinse the chicken carcasses well under cold running water. Roughly chop all the vegetables and put in a pan with the bones. Bring to the boil and skim. Simmer for 3–4 hours. Strain. If you want a dark chicken stock, bake the carcasses in the oven at 180 °C/350 °F for 45 minutes before putting them in the stock.

Al dente:
When vegetables, pasta, rice etc. are not completely cooked through but are still firm in the middle.

Agar agar:
Jelly powder made from seaweed. The powder can withstand heat, up to 75 °C/170 °F.

Biffsnadder:
Strips of steak.

Blanching:
Immersing briefly in boiling water, then plunging in ice water.

Clipfish:
Dried, salted cod.

Coulis:
A sauce made of berries or fruits with added sugar.

Curry:
This is a description applied to spice mixtures from many different Asian countries. There are many thousands of different recipes. In Thailand they have fresher curries made with fresh herbs and spices like green curry, while in India many curries are heavier and made mainly with dried spices such as garam masala.

Flensburger:
Ice cream with warm berries and egg liqueur.

Galangal:
A root frequently used in Thailand and other South-east Asian countries. Ginger can be used as a substitute, but galangal is more aromatic.

Glazing:
Covering something that has almost finished cooking with a fairly thick liquid that will cling when you pour it over, just before serving.

Hippen:
Thin, crispy biscuits for decorating desserts.

Joconde:
A thin cake used around the outside of desserts to give a pretty pattern and a "perfect" look.

Komler:
Norwegian potato dumplings.

Lapper:
Small pancakes.

Mandolin:
A utensil to help you cut thin slices of solid foods. The thickness can be adjusted.

Nage:
From the French verb nager, meaning to swim. This is a thin soup, often containing butter or oil.

Paellotto:
A word coined by the Norwegian chef Odd Sivar Solvold. It is a mixture of risotto and paella, as it contains the same ingredients as paella, but with the addition of Parmesan like a risotto.

Poaching:
Simmering in a liquid that is just below boiling point.

Portable smoker:
Portable smokers are really intended for outdoor use, but are quite often used in the kitchen. They consist of a steel "kettle" with a tight-fitting lid. Inside is a grid on which you place the food. You heat the smoker with wood chips until it begins to smoke.

Reducing:
Boiling a liquid so that the water evaporates and the liquid decreases in volume.

Sabayon:
An airy sauce made of eggs and wine. It is most commonly used in desserts, when it is known in English as zabaglione (Italian: zabaione). It is also used occasionally in savoury dishes, when butter is added, making it a bit like hollandaise sauce but airier.

Sautéing:
Lightly shallow frying in a pan (sauteuse), stirring occasionally.

Siphon:
An adaptation of the traditional soda siphon, which can be filled with liquids or creams. It uses pressurised gas cartridges, so when the contents are sprayed out they are aerated, so cream is "whipped" and liquids are fizzy. El Bulli in Spain introduced it to the kitchen and it has become very popular over the last twenty years.

Soufflé:
A light, airy mixture that expands above the mould in which it is made. It may be hot or cold, baked or an ice soufflé.

Vinaigrette:
A sauce containing vinegar, oil and seasonings, used on salads and vegetables to add extra flavour.

INTERNAL TEMPERATURES:
Here is a list of my "ultimate" internal temperatures. This is
what the temperature should be inside the meat when it has
rested. The temperature rises by at least 10% during resting.
If the meat is at 55 °C/130 °F when you take it out, the
temperature will be over 60 °C/140°F after it has rested.

LAMB	62 °C/144 °F
VEAL	59 °C/138 °F
BEEF	56 °C/132 °F
CHICKEN/TURKEY	62 °C/144 °F
PORK	62 °C/144 °F
DUCK	59 °C/138 °F
COD	56 °C/132 °F
SALMON	46 °C/115 °F
HALIBUT	48 °C/118 °F
POLLOCK	55 °C/130 °F

BREAD 95 °C/149 °F
– in this case, this should be the temperature when you take it
out of the oven, not after it has rested.

I would like to thank everyone who has supported me and helped on the way to winning the Bocuse d'Or and becoming who I am now. The person who has meant most to me professionally is undoubtedly Odd Ivar Solvold. Without all his help, creativity and support, I would never have won the Bocuse d'Or and become the kind of chef I am now. Thank you very much Odd Ivar, and good luck with your new life.

Of course many other people have been involved from my childhood to the Bocuse d'Or.

Mum and Dad, who let me do things in the kitchen and answered all my questions; Granny from whom I got a lot of good cake recipes; Gerd in the school kitchen; the chefs at the Fjordhotel who taught me the first "kitchen tricks"; Solveig, Liv Karin and Sigmund at the domestic Science College, who always provided opportunities for continuing development and inspiration; Kjetil and Andre at Finnegaardsstuene and Jans Mat og Vinhus who, with their enormous enthusiasm for the job, steered me in the direction of "gourmet food"; Bård and Daniel at Solsiden, where I learned to make good food for huge numbers of people (whom we didn't know) every day; Trond at Le Canard with his classic French duck liver and whole roast duck; the bothers Koch for initiating me into the art of Danish cooking in Århus; Arne at Skarsnuten for his energy and ideas; all my colleagues in the national cooking team for two great years with gelatine and good spirits; the kind sponsors who made it possible for me to get where I wanted in the Bocuse d'Or; Johan for his good design for dishes and plates which add the finishing touch; Harald and Britt for Katrine, lots of good food and sewing; Kai and Jon Filip for the effort they put into washing up and other chores; Victor for always being someone I could rely on at Midtåsen when I was training and for helping us to do things perfectly every time; the ever-obliging "supertasters"

and critics Harald, Eyvind, Bent, Tom Victor (there won't be any more crates of beer now) and Henrik; Fredrik for relaxing with diving, shooting and skiing, and of course all my friends on Fitjar for lots of fun from my childhood through to the Bocuse d'Or. Sindre, you are sorely missed. Rock on!

THE COMPETITION "SLAVES":
Ørjan is the one who put up with it longest and participated in two of the most important competitions as a commis chef – Chef of the Year 2007 and the Bocuse d'Or Europe – and as general factotum and "veteran support" for Adrian in the Bocuse d'Or. Always positive, even after many days working 18 hours when things didn't all go right for us.

Karl Erik spreads cheerfulness and is always full of energy and humour. Important to have you with us on the days when it's a bit hard to get things done. Always helps with washing up, carrying, peeling, organising and food for the crew.

Adrian was the newest recruit to the Bocuse d'Or "garage". Involved in the Bocuse d'Or for four months and lived in the garage. A perfectionist, who likes things to be systematic and organised. Always wants to do things better, and did it best of all in Lyon.

Katrine has been my most important support and critic for the last five years. Always completely honest, whether it was a question of poor garnishes or … Full of high spirits and energy, which helps me when things are not going too well. Hope we'll have many more great years together. Thank you, you mean more to me than you think.

Geir Skeie